The BIG WASHINGTON REPRODUCIBLE Activity Book!

BY CAROLE MARSH

This activity book has material which correlates with Washington's Essential Academic Learning Requirements in History, Civics, Geography, and Economics.

At every opportunity, we have tried to relate information to the History and Social Science, English, Science, Math, Civics, Economics, and Computer Technology Washington directives.

For additional information, go to our websites:
www.washingtonexperience.com or **www.gallopade.com**.

Correlates with Washington's
EALR
Essential Academic
Learning Requirements

GALLOPADE INTERNATIONAL

Reading
R R
Reference Research
R R
Reinforcement

The Big Activity Book Team

Billie Walburn

Michael Marsh

Antoinette Miller

Michele Yother

Carole Marsh

Steven Saint-Laurent

Bob Longmeyer

Kathy Zimmer

Chad Beard

Cranston Davenport

Shery Kearney

Sherry Moss

Cecil Anderson

Pat Newman

Jackie Clayton

Terry Briggs

Victoria DeJoy

Al Fortunatti

Pam Dufresne

Gallopade is proud to be a member of these educational organizations and associations:

Published by

GALLOPADE™
INTERNATIONAL

800-536-2GET
www.gallopade.com

SHOPA MEMBER™
School, Home, & Office Products Association

NSSEA

ASCD

The Washington Experience Series

My First Pocket Guide to Washington!

The Washington Coloring Book!

My First Book About Washington!

Washington Jeopardy: Answers and Questions About Our State

Washington "Jography!": A Fun Run Through Our State

The Washington Experience! Sticker Pack

The Washington Experience! Poster/Map

Discover Washington CD-ROM

Washington "GEO" Bingo Game

Washington "HISTO" Bingo Game

A Word From The Author

Washington is a very special state. Almost everything about Washington is interesting and fun! It has a remarkable history that helped create the great nation of America. Washington enjoys an amazing geography of incredible beauty and fascination. The state's people are unique and have accomplished many great things.

This Activity Book is chock-full of activities to entice you to learn more about Washington. While completing puzzles, coloring activities, word codes, and other fun-to-do activities, you'll learn about your state's history, geography, people, places, animals, legends, and more.

Whether you're sitting in a classroom, stuck inside on a rainy day, or–better yet–sitting in the back seat of a car touring the wonderful state of Washington, my hope is that you have as much fun using this Activity Book as I did writing it.

Enjoy your Washington Experience–it's the trip of a lifetime!!

Carole Marsh

Geographic Tools

Beside each geographic need listed, put the initials of the tool that can best help you!

(CR) Compass Rose   (LL) Longitude and Latitude
(M) Map   (G) Grid
(K) Map key/legend

1. _____ I need to find the geographic location of Germany.

2. _____ I need to learn where an airport is located near Seattle.

3. _____ I need to find which way is north.

4. _____ I need to chart a route from Washington to California.

5. _____ I need to find a small town on a map.

Match the items on the left with the items on the right.

1. Grid system
2. Compass rose
3. Longitude and latitude
4. Two of Washington's borders
5. Symbols on a map

A. Map key or legend
B. Oregon and Ohio
C. A system of letters and numbers
D. Imaginary lines around the earth
E. Shows N, S, E, and W

ANSWERS: 1-LL; 2-K; 3-CR; 4-M; 5-G; 1-C; 2-E; 3-D; 4-B; 5-A

An Apple a Day!

More apples are grown in Washington than any other state. Apples grow everywhere in Washington, both east and west of the Cascade Mountains. The best known apples are the Red Delicious and Gold Delicious, but more than 20 different varieties are grown in the state.

The first apple tree was planted in Washington in 1826 at Fort Vancouver. In 1854, the first orchard was begun near Oroville. By 1910, Washington was the nation's leading apple producer.

After planting, it takes two or three years before the tree bears fruit. A tree can produce apples for 20 to 30 years and can produce up to 20 boxes of apples each year.

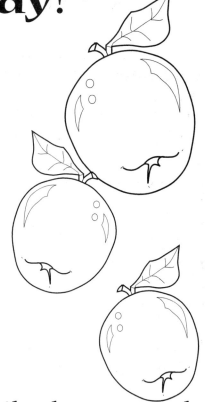

Answer the questions from the information in the above paragraphs.

1. How many different varieties of apples are grown in Washington?

   _____

2. Where was the first apple tree in Washington planted?

   _____

3. How many boxes of apples can a tree produce each year?

   _____

4. What are the best known varieties of apples?

   _____

5. How many years can a tree produce apples?

   _____

ANSWERS: 1-more than 20; 2-Fort Vancouver; 3-20; 4-Red Delicious and Gold Delicious; 5-20-30 years

Washington Government

Washington's state government, just like our national government, is made up of three branches. Each branch has a certain job to do. Each branch also has some power over the other branches. We call this system checks and balances. The three branches work together to make our government work smoothly.

EXECUTIVE	LEGISLATIVE	JUDICIAL
This branch includes the governor, lieutenant governor, secretary of state, attorney general, state treasurer, state auditor, superintendent of public instruction, insurance commissioner, and commissioner of public lands. It makes sure the laws are enforced.	This branch is made up of two houses, the Senate (49 members) and the House of Representatives (98 members). This branch makes and repeals laws.	This branch includes the Supreme Court, which has nine justices. Lesser courts include court of appeals, district superior courts, and justice-of-the-peace courts. This branch interprets the law.
Executive Branch	**Legislative Branch**	**Judicial Branch**

For each of these government officials, circle whether he or she is part of the EXECUTIVE, the LEGISLATIVE, or the JUDICIAL branch.

1. the governor   EXECUTIVE   LEGISLATIVE   JUDICIAL

2. speaker of the state House of Representatives   EXECUTIVE   LEGISLATIVE   JUDICIAL

3. a state senator   EXECUTIVE   LEGISLATIVE   JUDICIAL

4. attorney general   EXECUTIVE   LEGISLATIVE   JUDICIAL

5. secretary of state   EXECUTIVE   LEGISLATIVE   JUDICIAL

6. probate court judge   EXECUTIVE   LEGISLATIVE   JUDICIAL

7. chief justice of the Washington Supreme Court   EXECUTIVE   LEGISLATIVE   JUDICIAL

8. a local district representative   EXECUTIVE   LEGISLATIVE   JUDICIAL

9. the lieutenant governor   EXECUTIVE   LEGISLATIVE   JUDICIAL

10. a superior court judge   EXECUTIVE   LEGISLATIVE   JUDICIAL

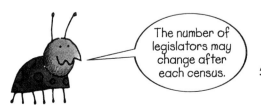

The number of legislators may change after each census.

ANSWERS: 1-executive; 2-legislative; 3-executive; 4-executive; 5-executive; 6-judicial; 7-judicial; 8-legislative; 9-executive; 10-judicial

All Around Washington! Bubblegram

Fill in the bubblegram by using the clues below.

1. Columbia River trading post established by Hudson's Bay Company
2. Strait located north of the Olympic Peninsula
3. Highest mountain in Washington
4. Sound located east of the Olympic Peninsula
5. A state south of Washington
6. Columbia River dam which created Franklin D. Roosevelt Lake

1. FORT ◯ _ _ _ _ _ _ _ ◯

2. _ _ _ _ _ ◯ _ _ _ _

3. _ _ _ _ _ _ _ _ _ _ ◯

4. _ _ ◯ _ _

5. _ _ ◯ _ ◯

6. _ _ _ _ _ _ _ _ ◯ ◯

Now unscramble the "bubble" letters to find out the mystery word!

Hint: Washington is known as the _____ State.

MYSTERY WORD: _ _ _ _ _ _ _ _ _

Lighting Up Washington!

Since the first one was built in 1856, lighthouses have played an important part in Washington's coastal history. The lights helped, and still help, guide ships and their crews along the Pacific Coast and through the dangers of Washington's inland waters.

The U.S. Lighthouse Service originally operated the lighthouses. In the 1930s, the lighthouses became the responsibility of the U.S. Coast Guard. When the lighthouses were first built, lightkeepers kept the lights burning. Today, most lighthouses are automated, and many are open to the public.

Lightships are anchored ships that serve as a lighthouse in places where a fixed structure can't be built. The lightships mark dangerous shoals and reefs!

Solve these rebuses (word puzzles with letter and picture clues) to find out the names of Washington's lighthouses.

1. Visitors can tour one of these at Lake Union in Seattle!

 _____

2. The last lighthouse in Washington to be automated is located on Elliot Bay in Puget Sound near Seattle. It was built in 1881 and was automated in 1984.

 _____

3. Point No Point Lighthouse is located in the town of Hansville on this peninsula.

 _____

4. Washington's oldest lighthouse is three miles west of Ilwaco, near Fort Canby State Park. Its construction was delayed when the ship carrying its building materials sank just offshore in 1853.

_____

Washington Wheel of Fortune, Indian Style!

The names of Washington's many Native American tribes contain enough consonants to play . . . Wheel of Fortune!

See if you can figure out the Wheel of Fortune-style puzzles below! "Vanna" has given you some of the consonants in each word.

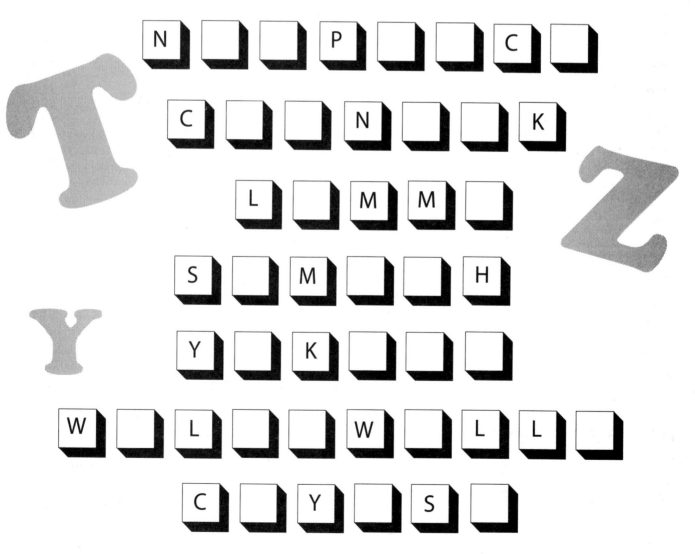

Rainbow, Pretty Rainbow

Rainbows often appear over the Nisqually River after a storm. Rainbows are formed when sunlight bends through raindrops. Big raindrops produce the brightest, most beautiful rainbows. You can see rainbows early or late on a rainy day when the sun is behind you.

Color the rainbow in the order the colors are listed below, starting at the top of the rainbow. Then, in each band write down as many Washington-related words as you can think of that begin with the same first letter as that color!

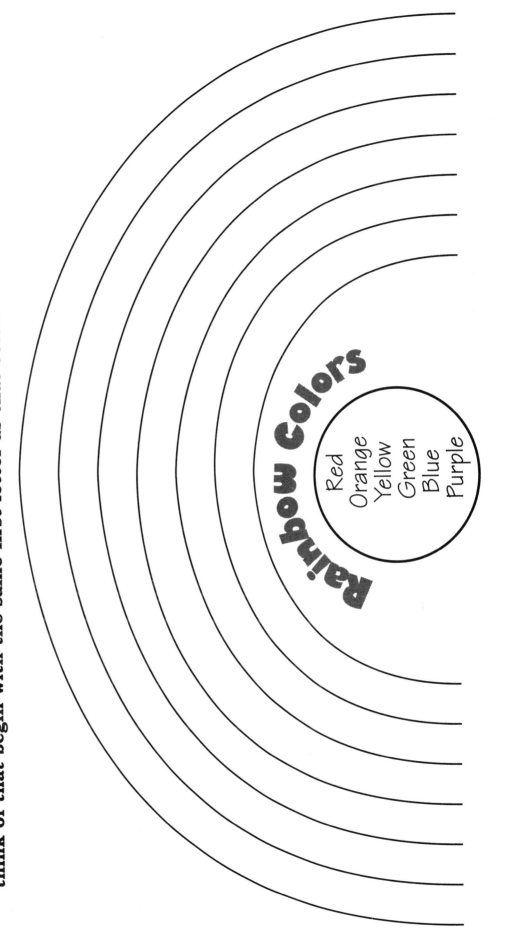

Rainbow Colors

Red
Orange
Yellow
Green
Blue
Purple

In the Beginning... There was a Settlement

In 1791, Spanish settlers founded the first European settlement in Washington on Neah Bay. The settlement was abandoned after five months. The United States, Great Britain, Spain, and Russia all laid claim to Oregon Country, the land that became the states of Washington and Oregon. The name *Oregon* comes from the French word *ouragan* which means "storm" or "hurricane."

Help the Spanish find their way to Neah Bay!

NEAH BAY

Finish

Start

U.S. Time Zones

Would you believe that the contiguous United States is divided into four time zones? It is! Because of the rotation of the earth, the sun appears to travel from east to west. Whenever the sun is directly overhead, we call that time noon. When it is noon in Philadelphia, Pennsylvania, the sun has a long way to go before it is directly over Seattle. When it is 12:00 p.m. (noon) in Spokane, it is 10:00 a.m. in Chicago, Illinois. There is a one-hour time difference between each zone!

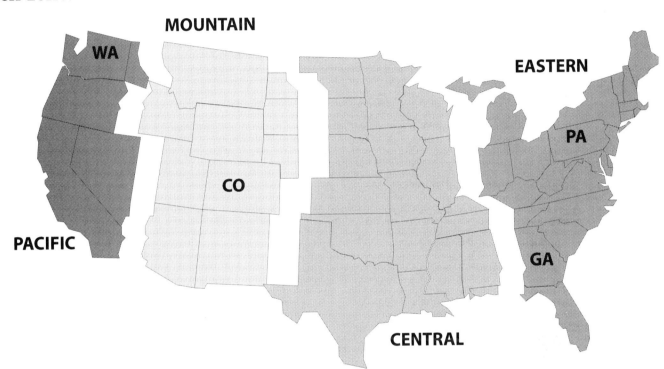

Look at the time zones on the map below, then answer the following questions:

1. When it is 10:00 a.m. in Walla Walla, Washington, what time is it in California? _____ a.m.

2. When it is 3:30 p.m. in Atlanta, Georgia, what time is it in Washington? _____ p.m.

3. In what time zone is Washington located? _____

4. In what time zone is Colorado located? _____

5. If it is 10:00 p.m. in Bellevue, Washington, what time is it in Alabama? _____ p.m.

ANSWERS: 1- 10:00 a.m.; 2-12:30 p.m.; 3-Pacific; 4-Mountain; 5-8:00 p.m.

Sing Like a Washington Bird Word Jumble

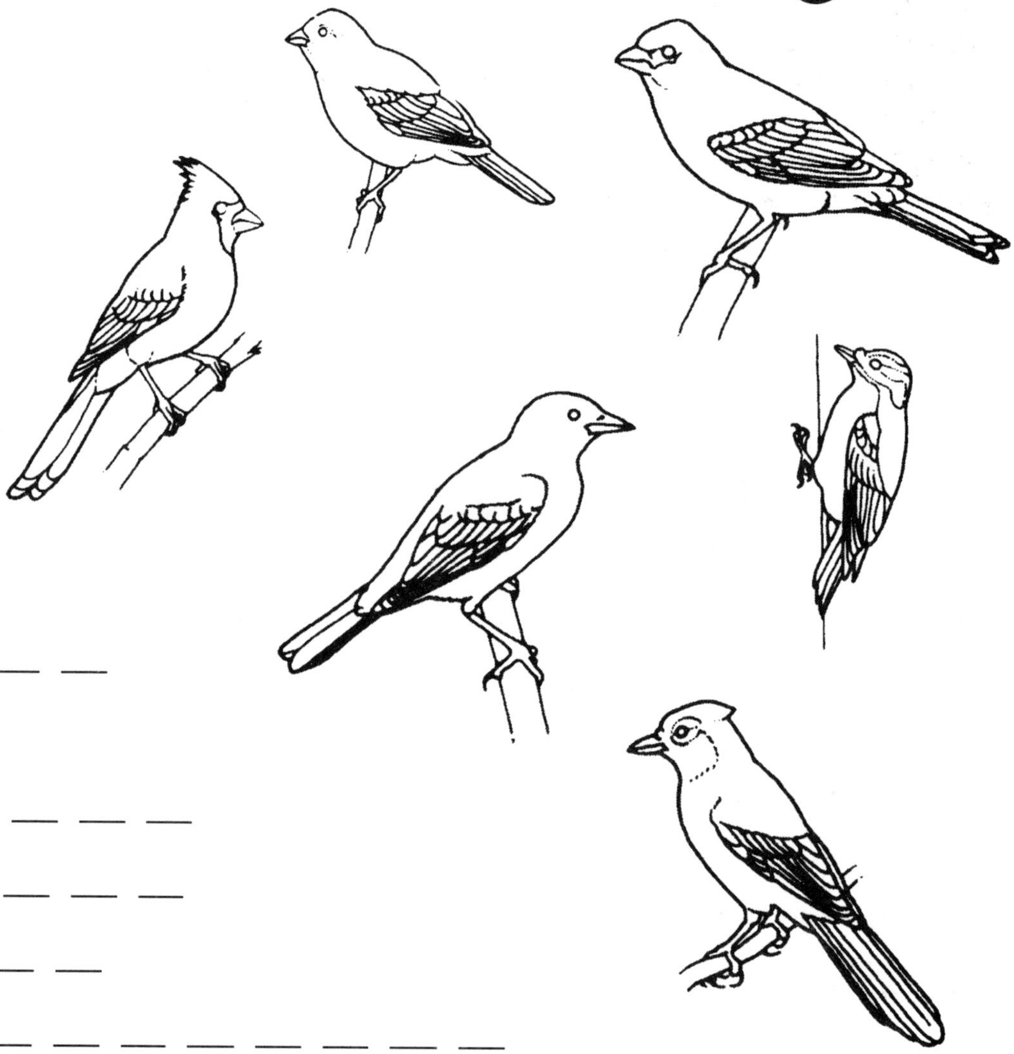

Oystercatcher
Goose
Owl
Hawk
Willow Goldfinch
Pelican
Pheasant
Quail
Ruffed Grouse
Duck

k c u d __ __ __ __

l o w __ __ __

o s e o g __ __ __ __ __

l q i a u __ __ __ __ __

w a h k __ __ __ __

t s a p e h a n __ __ __ __ __ __ __ __

d e r f u f s e g r o u __ __ __ __ __ __ __ __ __ __ __ __ __

l e p a c i n __ __ __ __ __ __ __

i w o l w l g o h n i f c l d

__ __ __ __ __ __ __ __ __ __ __ __ __ __ __ __

r c a e r s t t e o y c h

__ __ __ __ __ __ __ __ __ __ __ __ __

ANSWERS: duck; owl; goose; quail; hawk; pheasant; ruffed grouse; pelican; willow goldfinch; oystercatcher

Washington Schools Rule!

Washington's first school opened at Fort Vancouver in 1832. It was started by employees of the Hudson's Bay Company for their children. The state's public school system includes more than 2,000 schools in 298 public school districts and colleges and universities. Washington has six public and 18 private colleges and universities, 29 community colleges, and five technical schools.

Complete the names of these Washington schools. Use the Word Bank to help you. Then, use the answers to solve the code at the bottom.

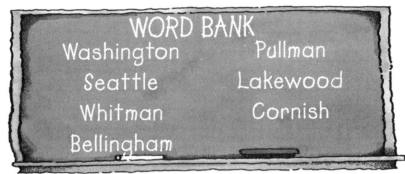

WORD BANK
Washington   Pullman
Seattle   Lakewood
Whitman   Cornish
Bellingham

1. Central __ __ __ __ __ __ __ __ __ University in Ellensburg
                2

2. University of Washington in __ __ __ __ __ __ __
                                      4

3. Washington State University in __ __ __ __ __ __ __
                                    3

4. __ __ __ __ __ __ __ College of the Arts in Seattle
      5

5. Pierce College in __ __ __ __ __ __ __ __
                                        1

6. __ __ __ __ __ __ __ College in Walla Walla
              7

7. Western Washington University in __ __ __ __ __ __ __ __ __ __ __
                                                                  6

The coded message tells you what all college students want!

__ __ __ __ __ __ __
1 2 3 4 5 6 7

Washington Topography is "Tops"!

When we learn about Washington's topography, we use special words to describe it. These words describe the things that make each part of the state interesting.

Cross out every other letter below beginning with the first one to find out what each topographical term is!

1. **P S A T B R Z A R I X T:** a narrow body of water that joins two larger bodies of water

2. **R P A E B N C I S N T S R U X L L A:** a long piece of land nearly surrounded by water

3. **Z S Y O X U W N U D:** a long, wide arm of a sea, or a channel between an island and a mainland

4. **R M A O I U N N I T E A R I T N:** a very high peak or hill

5. **M V O O U L N C T A A N I O:** an opening in the earth's crust, often at the top of a mountain, from which lava escapes

6. **G C R O A U N L D E E E:** a deep canyon formed by rain and melting snow

7. **C P O L L A U T M E B A I U:** a mountain or hill with a level top

8. **P T U R G O E U T G O H:** a long narrow hollow in the surface of a sea bed or the ground

9. **R V I A V L E L R E S Y:** a low area of land with a river or stream running through it that is surrounded by higher land

10. **N G O L W A Y C S I K E I R:** a large body of ice and snow formed in mountain valleys, or the North and South Poles, which moves slowly

ANSWERS: 1-strait; 2-peninsula; 3-sound; 4-mountain; 5-volcano; 6-coulee; 7-plateau; 8-trough; 9-valley; 10-glacier

Oh! Say Can You See...
The Washington State Flag

The state of Washington was named after George Washington, the first president of the United States. Washington is the only state named after a president. Washington's current state flag was adopted in 1923. It features the state seal centered on a dark green field. George Washington's picture is featured on the state seal.

Color the state flag.

Design your own Diamante on Washington!

A *diamante* is a cool diamond-shaped poem on any subject.

You can write your very own diamante poem on Washington by following the simple line by line directions below. Give it a try!

Line 1:   Write the name of your state.

Line 2:   Write the names of two animals native to your state.

Line 3:   Write the names of three important cities in your state.

Line 4:   Write the names of the state bird and the state tree.

Line 5:   Write the name of volcano that erupted in your state in 1980.

Line 6:   Write the name of state dance.

Line 7:   Write the word that completes this sentence: Washington's nickname is the _____ State.

_____

_____ _____

_____ _____ _____

_____ _____ _____ _____ _____

_____ _____ _____

_____ _____

_____

YOU'RE a poet!
Did you know it?

History Mystery Tour!

Washington is bursting at the seams with history! Here are just a few of the many historical sites that you might visit. Try your hand at locating them on the map! **Draw a symbol for each site on the Washington map below.**

Claquato Church, Chehalis—oldest church in the state, built in 1858

George E. Pickett House, Bellingham—built in 1856 for Pickett, who later led the Confederate charge at the Battle of Gettysburg

Fort Nisqually, DuPont—reconstruction of post built in 1833 by Hudson's Bay Company

San Juan Island National Historic Park—honors the bloodless dispute that occurred when both the United States and Great Britain claimed San Juan Island

Whitman Mission National Historical Site, near Walla Walla—honors the Indian mission founded by Marcus and Narcissa Whitman in 1836

Monticello Convention Site, Longview—location where Washington residents petitioned the federal government to separate Washington from Oregon

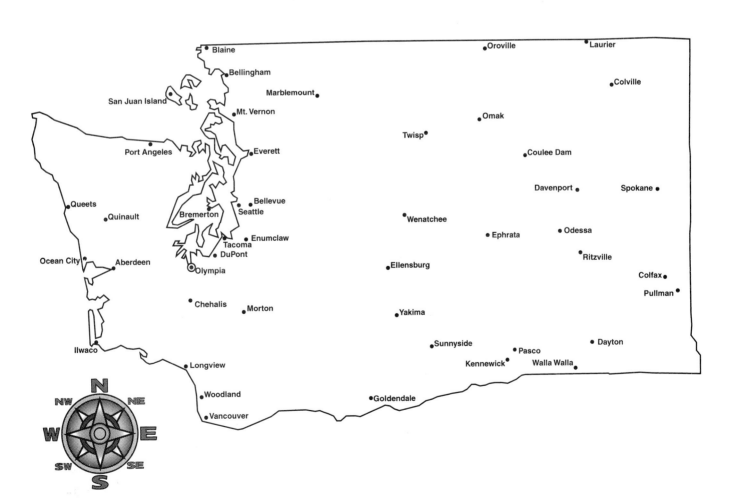

What in the World?

A hemisphere is one-half of a sphere (globe) created by the prime meridian or equator. Every place in the world is in two hemispheres (Northern or Southern and Eastern or Western). The equator is an imaginary line that runs around the world from left to right and divides the globe into the Northern Hemisphere and the Southern Hemisphere. The prime meridian is an imaginary line that runs around the world from top to bottom and divides the globe into the Eastern Hemisphere and Western Hemisphere.

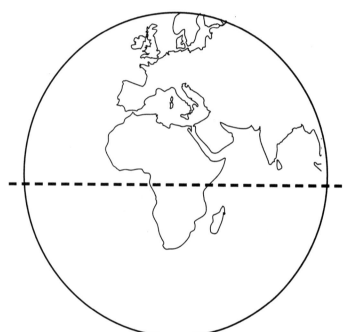

Label the Northern and Southern Hemispheres.

Write E on the equator.

Is Washington in the NORTHERN or SOUTHERN Hemisphere? (circle one)

Color the map.

Label the Eastern and Western Hemispheres.

Write PM on the prime meridian.

Is Washington in the EASTERN or WESTERN Hemisphere? (circle one)

Color the map.

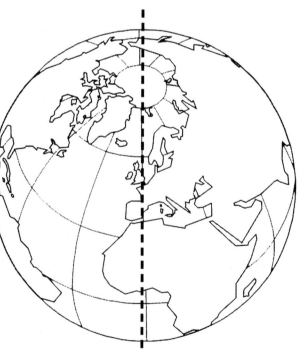

Places to go! Things to do!

Washington has so many cool places to go and so many cool things to do! **Use the Word Bank to help you complete the sentences below and learn about some of the exciting Washington sites you can visit!**

1. ___ ___ ___ ___ ___ Arch State Park in Blaine is a six-story arch on the U.S./Canadian border which commemorates the countries' friendship.

2. Olympic Game ___ ___ ___ ___ in Sequim is home to exotic animals that have retired from show business.

3. Hells ___ ___ ___ ___ ___ ___ on the Snake River in southeastern Washington is the deepest canyon in the continental United States.

4. Cat Tales ___ ___ ___ ___ ___ ___ ___ ___ ___ ___ Species Conservation Park in Mead is home to more than two dozen big cats.

5. The Space Needle in ___ ___ ___ ___ ___ ___ ___ is a 607-foot (185-meter) observation tower built for the 1962 World's Fair.

6. Stonehenge in Maryhill is a ___ ___ ___ ___ ___ ___ ___ ___ to soldiers who died in World War I.

7. Mount St. Helens National ___ ___ ___ ___ ___ ___ ___ ___ Monument is near Castle Rock.

8. Fort ___ ___ ___ ___ ___ ___ near White Swan was built in 1856 during the Yakima War.

WORD BANK

Peace	canyon	Simcoe	Endangered
memorial	Volcanic	Farm	Seattle

ANSWERS: 1-Peace; 2-Farm; 3-Canyon; 4-Endangered; 5-Seattle; 6-memorial; 7-Volcanic; 8-Simcoe

Please Come to Washington!

You have a friend who lives in North Dakota. She is thinking of moving to Washington because she wants to work on a ferry boat, and Washington has the largest ferry system in the United States.

Write her a letter describing Washington and some of the ferry boat crew opportunities here.

Washington State Ferries (WSF), a state-operated system, carries more than 70,000 people a day on Puget Sound ferry routes. WSF has 20 terminals located in eight of Washington's counties and in British Columbia. Some of the ferries carry automobiles and some are for passengers only. In addition, WSF runs a ferry in eastern Washington on the Columbia River. There are also several private and small public ferries which operate throughout the state.

Majestic Mount Rainier

Mount Rainier in the Cascade Mountains is Washington's highest peak at 14,410 feet (4,392 meters) and the highest volcano in the United States. It is a dormant volcano, which means it isn't extinct, but it isn't erupting!

Mount Rainier has 34 square miles (88 square kilometers) of glaciers and is the largest glacial system on a single peak in the United States outside of Alaska.

The Native Americans call Mount Rainier *Tahoma* which means "Mountain that was God."

Congress established Mount Rainier National Park in 1899. The visitors center and park headquarters is located at Longmire. Mount Rainier is home to 62 major lakes, 30 large waterfalls, and more than 700 different species of flowering plants!

Use information from the story above to complete the crossword.

1. Mount Rainier National Park headquarters is located at _____. (ACROSS)

2. Mount Rainier is in the _____ Mountains. (ACROSS)

3. Mount Rainier has 34 square miles (88 square kilometers) of _____. (DOWN)

4. _____ is the name Native Americans call Mount Rainier. (ACROSS)

5. Mount Rainier is a _____ volcano. (DOWN)

6. Mount Rainier is home to 30 waterfalls and 62 major _____. (ACROSS)

ANSWERS: 1-Longmire; 2-Cascade; 3-glaciers; 4-Tahoma; 5-dormant; 6-lakes

©2001 Carole Marsh/Gallopade International/800-536-2GET/www.washingtonexperience.com/Page 23

Washington Rules!

Fast facts

A workmen's compensation bill was approved in 1911.

In 1912, the state legislature approves a bill that gave direct power to voters to enact new laws or change existing laws.

In 1917, a medical act set up a fund to help injured workers. Both workers and employers contribute.

Washington established a Department of Health in 1921.

Washington established a court of appeals with 12 judges who are elected for six-year terms in 1969.

Use the code to complete the sentences.

A	B	C	D	E	F	G	H	I	J	K	L	M	N	O	P
1	2	3	4	5	6	7	8	9	10	11	12	13	14	15	16

Q	R	S	T	U	V	W	X	Y	Z
17	18	19	20	21	22	23	24	25	26

1. State rules are called __ __ __ __.
   12 1 23 19

2. Laws are made in our state __ __ __ __ __ __ __.
   3 1 16 9 20 15 12

3. The leader of our state is the __ __ __ __ __ __ __ __.
   7 15 22 5 18 14 15 18

4. We live in the state of __ __ __ __ __ __ __ __ __ __.
   23 1 19 8 9 14 7 20 15 14

5. The capital of our state is __ __ __ __ __ __ __.
   15 12 25 13 16 9 1

W A S H I N G T O N ! ! !

Buzzing Around Washington!

Write the answers to the questions below. To get to the beehive, follow a path through the maze.

1. The University of Washington in _____ was the first territorial university in the Pacific Northwest.

2. Eby's Landing National Historical Reserve on _____ _____ is a settlement founded in the 1850s.

3. _____ Gold Rush National Historical Park in Seattle is the southern part of a park located in Skagway, Alaska, which honors Seattle's role in the Gold Rush.

4. Fort Vancouver is a reconstruction of the western headquarters of _____.

5. The Yakama Nation Cultural Heritage Center in _____ features different types of lodges and dioramas of everyday Native American life.

6. The Whale Museum at Friday Harbor on _____ _____ _____ has whale skeletons and models.

7. Cape Disappointment Lighthouse in _____, built in 1856, is oldest in the Pacific Northwest.

8. Fort Nisqually in _____ is a reconstruction of a post built in 1833 by Hudson's Bay Company.

9. Seattle Aquarium offers an underwater view of _____ _____ sea life.

10. The old coal-mining town of _____ has 23 cemeteries and was the set for the television series *Northern Exposure*.

Seattle · Klondike · Start here · Whidbey Island · Puget Sound · Hudson's Bay Company · Roslyn · DuPont · Ilwaco · Toppendish · San Juan Island

ANSWERS: 1-Seattle; 2-Whidbey Island; 3-Klondike; 4-Hudson's Bay Company; 5-Toppendish; 6-San Juan Island; 7-Ilwaco; 8-DuPont; 9-Puget Sound; 10-Roslyn

Washington Through the Years!

Many great things have happened in Washington throughout its history. Chronicle the following important Washington events by solving math problems to find out the years in which they happened.

1. The coast of Washington and Puget Sound is surveyed by George Vancouver

   $6÷6=$ $5+2=$ $3x3=$ $8÷4=$

2. Meriwether Lewis and William Clark reach Washington and the Pacific Ocean

   $0+1=$ $4x2=$ $9-9=$ $10÷2=$

3. Washington's boundary set at 49th parallel in a treaty between United States and Britain

   $3÷3=$ $4+4=$ $2x2=$ $9-3=$

4. Congress creates Washington Territory

   $9-8=$ $2+6=$ $8-3=$ $3x1=$

5. Northern Pacific Railroad links Washington and the East

   $1x1=$ $7+1=$ $9-1=$ $3÷1=$

6. Washington becomes 42nd state

   $9÷9=$ $8x1=$ $5+3=$ $5+4=$

7. Grand Coulee Dam is completed

   $6-5=$ $8+1=$ $5-1=$ $2-0=$

8. World's fair, Century 21, held in Seattle

   $2÷2=$ $3x3=$ $3+3=$ $2-0=$

9. Mount St. Helen's erupts

   $4÷4=$ $7+2=$ $0+8=$ $8-8=$

10. Gary Locke becomes first Chinese-American elected governor of a continental U.S. state

    $9÷9=$ $6+3=$ $9x1=$ $8-2=$

ANSWERS: 1-1792; 2-1805; 3-1846; 4-1853; 5-1883; 6-1889; 7-1942; 8-1962; 9-1980; 10-1996

What Did We Do Before Money?

   In early Washington, there were no banks. However, people still wanted to barter, trade, or otherwise "purchase" goods from each other. Wampum, made of shells, bone, or stones, was often swapped for goods. Indians, especially, used wampum for "money." In the barter system, people swapped goods or services.

   The Chinook Indians were the greatest traders in the Pacific Northwest. Although the Indian tribes all spoke their own languages, most of them used Chinook words when they bartered. Tribes from throughout the Pacific Northwest gathered to trade at The Dalles on the Oregon side of the Columbia River.

   Later, banks came into existence, and people began to use money to buy goods. However, they also still bartered when they had no money to spend. **Place a star in the box below the systems used today.**

Rhymin' Riddles

1. We lived in Washington before the explorers did roam;
   On lands near rivers and lakes were our tribes' home.

   Who are we? _____

2. The hope of the Oregon Territory never did fail;
   To reach promised land, settlers followed this trail.

   What am I? _____ _____

3. Centralia is the name of the town I did claim;
   With our country's first president I share my name.

   Who am I? _____

4. When it comes to great fishing in Washington,
   I'm the prize catch;
   Yearly I return from saltwater to fresh, my eggs to hatch.

   What am I? _____

Washington Map Symbols

Make up symbols for these names and draw them in the space provided on the right.

cattle	
apples	
manufacturing	
airport	
hospital	
military installations	
ports	
forests	
camping	

Washington Goodies!

Match the name of each crop or product from Washington with the picture of that item.

apples   onions   grapes   asparagus   red raspberries   mint

Washington is first in the nation in the production of apples, red raspberries, mint, and asparagus.

Washington's state fruit is the apple.

Food processing is the largest manufacturing industry in Washington.

Walla Walla Sweet Onions are guaranteed not to make your eyes water when you cut them.

Historical Washington Women World Wonders!

Washington has been the home of many brave and influential women. See if you can match these women with their accomplishments.

1. Narcissa Prentiss Whitman

2. Mary Ann Boren Denny

3. Dixy Lee Ray

4. Sarah Winnemucca

5. Fay Fuller

6. Maude C. Lillie Bolin

7. Bertha Knight Landes

8. Dr. Nettie J. Craig Asberry

9. Lizzie Ordway

10. Mother Joseph

A. educator who started schools and fought for women's suffrage

B. first woman to climb Mount Rainier

C. music teacher and civil rights leader

D. she and her husband founded the settlement that became Seattle

E. elected mayor of Seattle in 1926, first woman mayor of major city in United States

F. first woman governor of Washington

G. spokeswoman for Indian rights

H. Catholic nun who established schools and hospitals

I. rodeo performer, civic leader; and pilot

J. she and her husband established a mission and were killed by the Cayuse Indians

ANSWERS: 1-J; 2-D; 3-F; 4-G; 5-B; 6-I; 7-E; 8-C; 9-A; 10-H

Producers and Consumers

Producers (sellers) make goods or provide services. Ralph, a 4th grade student in Toppenish, is a consumer because he wants to buy a new wheel for his bicycle. Other products and services from Washington that consumers can buy include airplanes, computers, ships, and wood products.

Fast Facts:
* Software is the fastest growing industry in Washington.
* Tourists bring billions of dollars to Washington each year.
* High-technology industries provide one-third of Washington's jobs.
* Washington is a major producer of waterpower and hydroelectricity (electricity generated by water).

Complete these sentences.

Without hydroelectricity, I couldn't

_____

_____

Without airplanes, I couldn't

_____

_____

Without ships, I couldn't

_____

_____

Without computers, I couldn't

_____

_____

Washington Word Wheel!

Use the Word Wheel of Washington names to complete the sentences below.

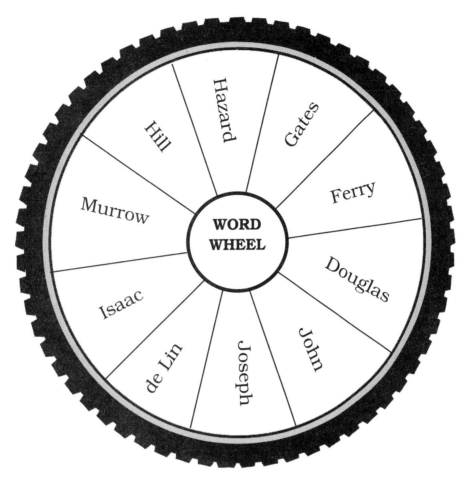

1. Scottish fur trader _____ McLoughlin founded the Hudson's Bay Company trading post at Fort Vancouver.

2. Swedish immigrant Nichalas _____ built the first water-driven sawmill in Tacoma in 1852.

3. William O. _____ served the longest term in history as a U.S. Supreme Court justice.

4. Bill _____ developed the first computer language for a personal computer.

5. News reporter Edmund R. _____ is considered the "Father of Television News."

6. Chief _____, a Nez Perce chief, tried to lead his people to safety in Canada after being told to move from Oregon to Idaho.

7. _____ Stevens was the first territorial governor of Washington.

8. _____ Stevens made the first recorded conquest of Mount Rainier.

9. Sam _____ designed and built the Peace Arch, the Stonehenge-style memorial to honor World War I soldiers, and the Maryhill Museum of Art.

10. Elisha P. _____ served as first governor of Washington.

A Blast from the Past!

Washington is bursting at the seams with history! Here are just a few of the many historical sites that you might visit. **Try your hand at locating them on the map! Draw the symbol for each site on the Washington map below.**

∗ **Whitman Mission National Historical Site:** Founded in 1836 near Walla Walla by Marcus and Narcissa Whitman, the Indian mission also served as a stop for settlers on the Oregon Trail. The diseases brought by the settlers killed many Indians which caused the Cayuse to attack the mission and kill the missionaries.

■ **Capital Campus:** Japanese cherry trees bloom on the grounds of the Capital Campus in Olympia which includes the capitol building, the justice building, as well as other administrative buildings of the state government.

▲ **Pioneer Square Historic District:** The oldest neighborhood in Seattle is an 18-block area of restored historic buildings. The neighborhood marked the center of town during the 19th century.

◆ **Dayton Depot:** Built in 1881, the Dayton Depot is the oldest existing railroad station in Washington. Dayton is home to the oldest courthouse, built in 1887, in the state still used by county government. The town also has 83 homes on the National Historic Register.

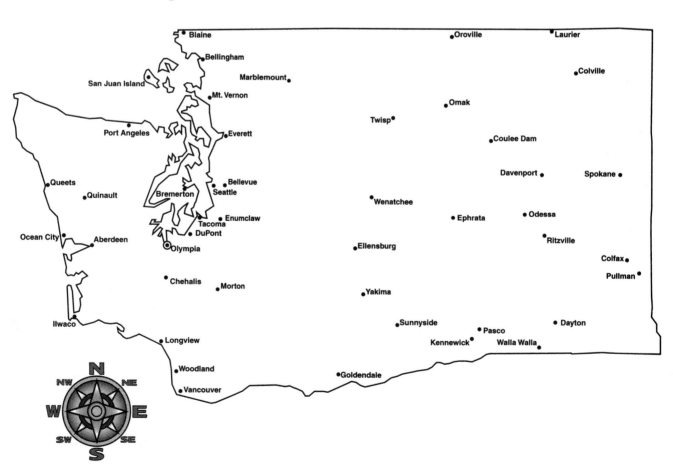

Create Your Own Washington State Quarter!

      Look at the change in your pocket. You might notice that one of the coins has changed. The United States is minting new quarters, one for each of the 50 states. Each quarter has a design on it that says something special about one particular state. The Washington quarter will be in cash registers and piggy banks everywhere after it's released in 2007.

What if you had designed the Washington quarter? Draw a picture of how you would like the Washington quarter to look. Make sure you include things that are special about Washington.

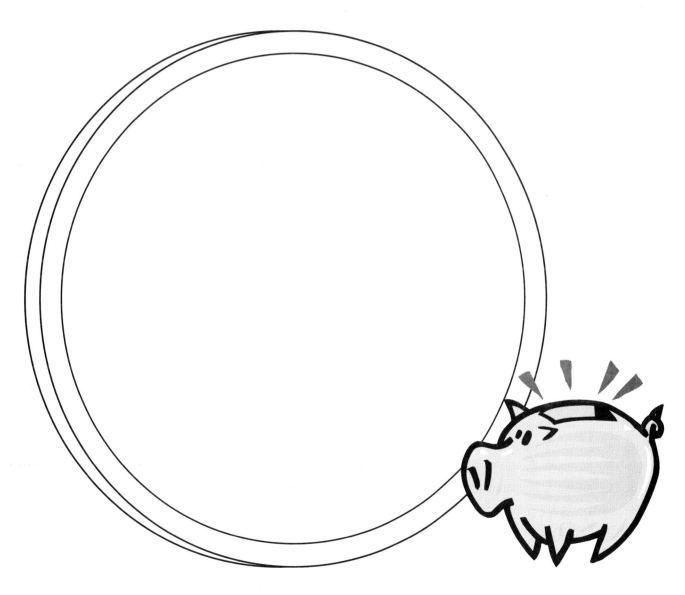

Washington Law Comes In Many Flavors!

For each of these people, write down the kind(s) of law used to decide whether their actions are legal or illegal.

1. Bank robber _____
2. Business person _____
3. State park ranger _____
4. Washingtonians _____
5. Doctor _____
6. Real estate agent _____
7. Corporate president _____
8. Ship owner _____
9. Diplomat _____
10. Soldier _____

Medical Law

International Law

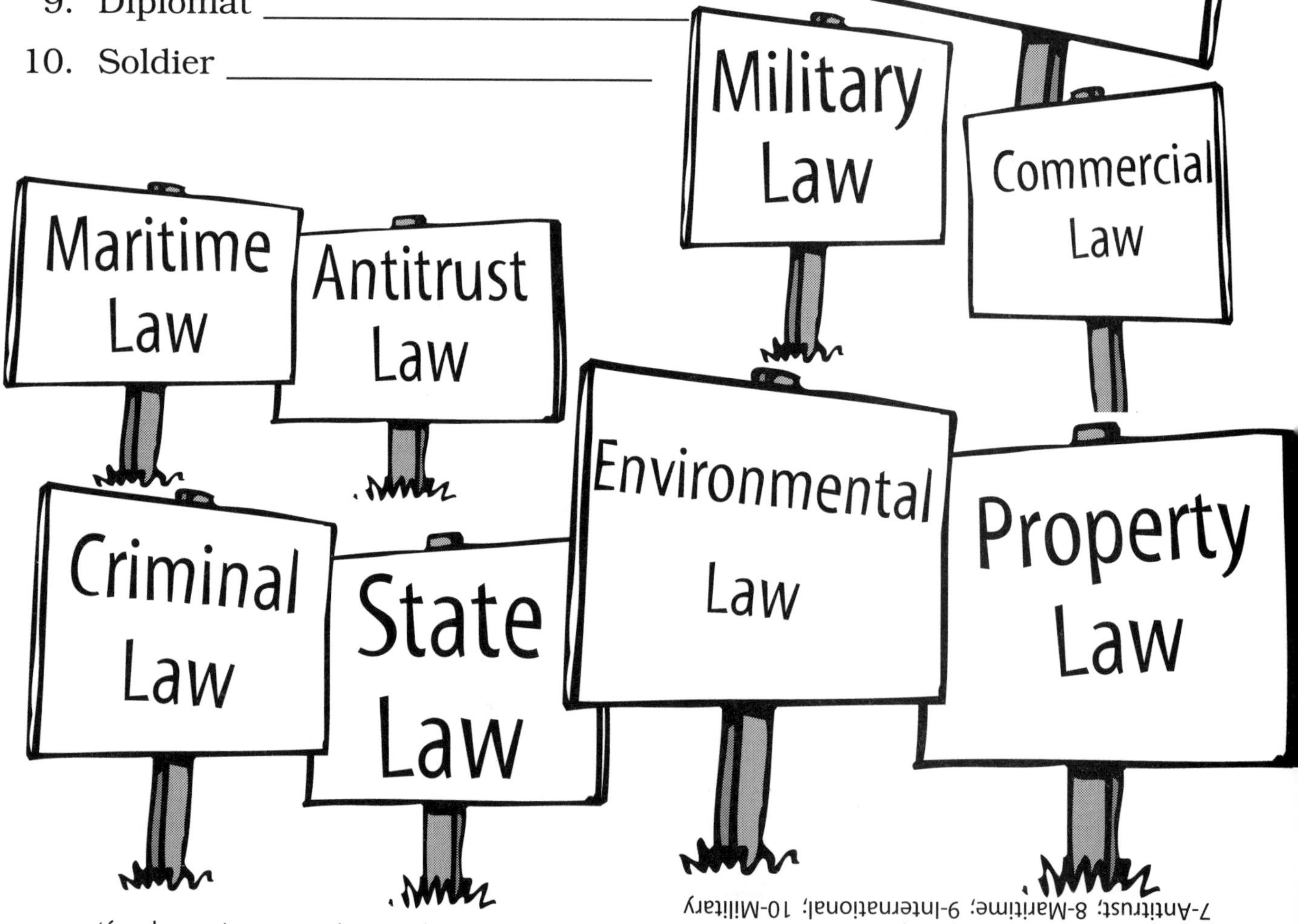

Military Law

Commercial Law

Maritime Law

Antitrust Law

Environmental Law

Property Law

Criminal Law

State Law

ANSWERS: (Answers may vary.) 1-Criminal; 2-Commercial; 3-Environmental; 4-State; 5-Medical; 6-Property; 7-Antitrust; 8-Maritime; 9-International; 10-Military

Mixed-Up States!

Color, cut out, and paste each of Washington's neighbors onto the map below.

Be sure and match the state shapes!

Oregon

Idaho

Washington

Building Boats in Bremerton, Seattle

Building and repairing ships is an important industry in Washington. The largest shipyard on the Pacific Coast is the Puget Sound Naval Shipyard in Bremerton. Dry docks for building and repairing ships are also found in Seattle, Tacoma, Bellingham, and Everett. Many Puget Sound ports also have small shipbuilding companies that build fishing and pleasure boats.

Seattle is the gateway of the Pacific Northwest to and from Asia, Alaska, and Hawaii. In addition to Seattle, major port cities include Tacoma, Anacortes, Bellingham, Longview, Kalama, and Vancouver.

When you're on board any kind of boat, you have to use special terms to talk about directions. Label the ship below with these terms:

bow: front of the ship
stern: back of the ship
fore: towards the bow
aft: towards the stern
port: left as you face the bow
starboard: right as you face the bow

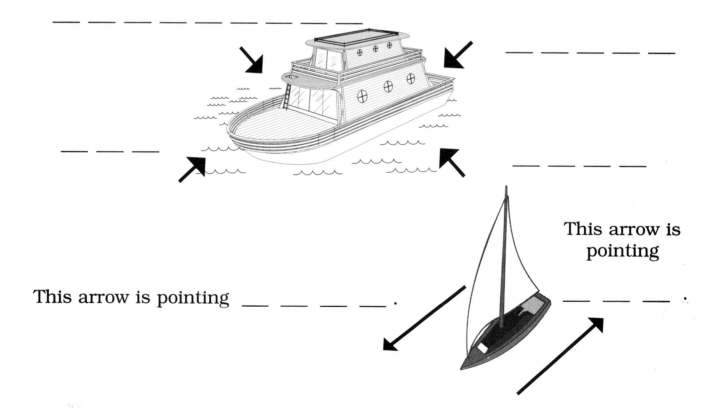

This arrow is pointing _ _ _ _ _ .

This arrow is pointing _ _ _ _ .

Washington Politics As Usual!

Our elected government officials decide how much money is going to be spent on schools, roads, public parks, and libraries. It's very important for the citizens of Washington to understand what's going on in their government, and how it will affect them.

Before the 19th Amendment to the U.S. Constitution, women were unable to vote in the United States. Some states began giving women the right to vote only in state elections. In 1910, Washington became the fifth state to grant woman the right to vote. In 1920, enough states ratified the 19th Amendment, and it became the law of the land. Women gained total suffrage nationally and continue to be a major force in the election process today.

On the lines provided, write down a question for each of the answers below. A hint follows each answer.

1. Question: _____

   Answer: A draft of a law presented for review.

   (Short for William!)

2. Question: _____

   Answer: The right to vote.

   (Don't make us suffer!)

3. Question: _____

   Answer: The ability to forbid a bill or law from being passed.

   (Just say no!)

4. Question: _____

   Answer: The fundamental law of the United States that was

   framed in 1787 and put into effect in 1789.

   (Washington has one too!)

5. Question: _____

   Answer: An amendment.

   (It's not something subtracted from #5!)

ANSWERS: (may vary slightly) 1-What is a bill? 2-What is suffrage? 3-What is a veto? 4-What is the Constitution? 5-What is an addition to the Constitution called?

What Shall I Be When I Grow Up?

Here are just a few of the jobs that kept early Washingtonians busy.

Lawyer	Barber	Jailer
Farmer	Gardener	Fisherman
Woodcarver	Dressmaker	Doctor
Judge	Printer	Governor
Housekeeper	Cook	Milliner (hatmaker)
Politician	Musician	Soldier
Dairyman	Bookbinder	Hunter
Wheelwright	Laundress	Blacksmith
Teacher	Jeweler	Sailor
Cabinetmaker	Innkeeper	Beekeeper
Mayor	Stablehand	Gunsmith
Cooper (barrelmaker)	Tailor	Prospector
Carpenter	Minister	Logger
Weaver	Baker	Shipbuilder

You are a young settlers trying to decide what you want to be when you grow up.

Choose a career and next to it write a description of what you think you would do each day as a:

Write your career choice here!

_____

Write your career choice here!

_____

Write your career choice here!

_____

Write your career choice here!

_____

Governor of Washington!

The governor is the leader of the state.

You've been assigned to write a biography of the governor of Washington.

Before you can start your book, you need to jot down some notes in your trusty computer. Fill in the necessary information in the spaces provided on the dossier!

GOVERNOR'S NAME:

_____

_____

Date of Birth:

Place of Birth:

Father:

Mother:

Siblings:

Spouse:

Children:

Pets:

Schools Attended:

Previous Occupation(s):

Likes:

Dislikes:

abc · APPLICATIONS MENU CALCULATOR FIND 123 ·

The ORIGINAL Native Washingtonians!

The Native Americans who lived west of the Cascade Mountains had rivers full of fish and forests with lots of deer, elk, and other game. They lived in red cedar longhouses.

East of the Cascades, the Native Americans moved often and lived in dugouts—shelters dug into the sides of hills and covered with grass mats. They fished, hunted wild game, and ate wild berries and roots.

What kinds of things did Native Americans use in their everyday life? For each of the things shown, circle YES if Native Americans did use it, or NO if they didn't.

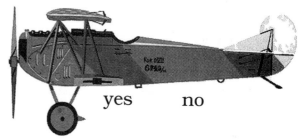

yes   no

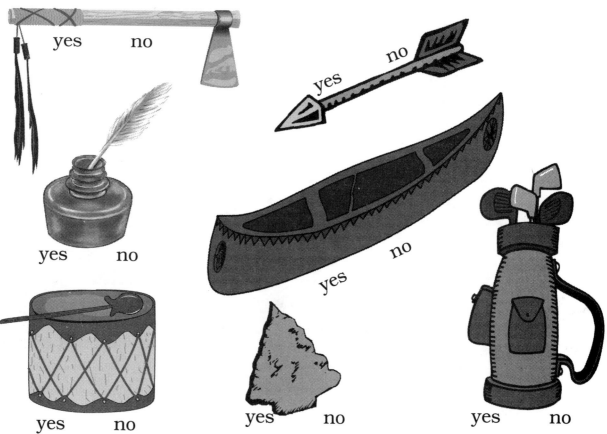

yes   no

yes   no

yes   no

yes   no

yes   no

yes   no

States All Around Code-Buster!

Decipher the code and write in the names of the states and provinces that border Washington.

A B C D E F G H I J K L M N O P Q R

S T U V W X Y Z

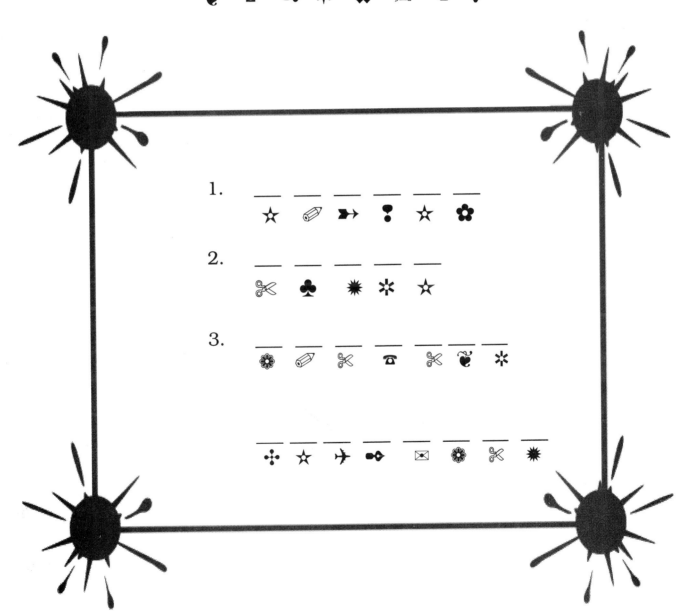

1. _ _ _ _ _ _

2. _ _ _ _ _

3. _ _ _ _ _ _ _

   _ _ _ _ _ _ _ _

Unique Washington Place Names!

Can you figure out the compound words that make up the names of these Washington places?

Appleton _____ _____

Bridgeport _____ _____

Dishman _____ _____

Edgewood _____ _____

Lakewood _____ _____

Longview _____ _____

Newcastle _____ _____

Newport _____ _____

Outlook _____ _____

Parkwater _____ _____

Seaview _____ _____

Springdale _____ _____

Startup _____ _____

Sunnyside _____ _____

Westport _____ _____

Looking For a Home in the Evergreen State!

Can you figure out where these things, people, and animals belong? Use the word clues to help you!

1. Tatoosh Island is home to the (RHYMES WITH APE) + (GIVING SOMEONE A COMPLIMENT)

   — — — — —   — — — — — — — — — — Lighthouse.

2. The Selkirk and Blue Mountains are home to Rocky Mountain (OPPOSITE OF SMALL+BRASS MUSICAL INSTRUMENT)

   — — — — — — — sheep.

3. Old-growth forests are home to (MARKED WITH SPOTS) + (BIRDS WHO ASKS "WHO?")

   — — — — — — — — — — — — — —.

4. Washington's inland waters are home to (SOMEONE WHO CAUSES THE DEATH OF ANOTHER) + (VERY LARGE SEA MAMMALS)

   — — — — — — — — — — — —.

5. (A LARGE BODY OF SALT WATER) + (LARGE MEMBER OF THE CAT FAMILY FOUND IN AFRICA)

   — — — — — — — — — can be found playing on the slippery rocks beneath the cliffs on the Washington shore.

ANSWERS: 1-Cape Flattery; 2-bighorn; 3-spotted owls; 4-killer whales; 5-sea lions

I Love Washington, Weather or Not!

The Cascade Mountains divide Washington into two different weather regions. Western Washington has mild, wet winters and cool summers. Eastern Washington is drier, hotter in the summer, and colder in the winter.

Washington's highest recorded temperature was 118°F (47.7°C) in Ice Harbor Dam in 1961. The lowest temperature recorded was -48°F (-44.4°C) in Mazama in 1968.

On the thermometer gauges below, color the mercury red (°F) to show the hottest temperature ever recorded in Washington. Color the mercury blue (°F) to show the coldest temperature ever recorded in Washington.

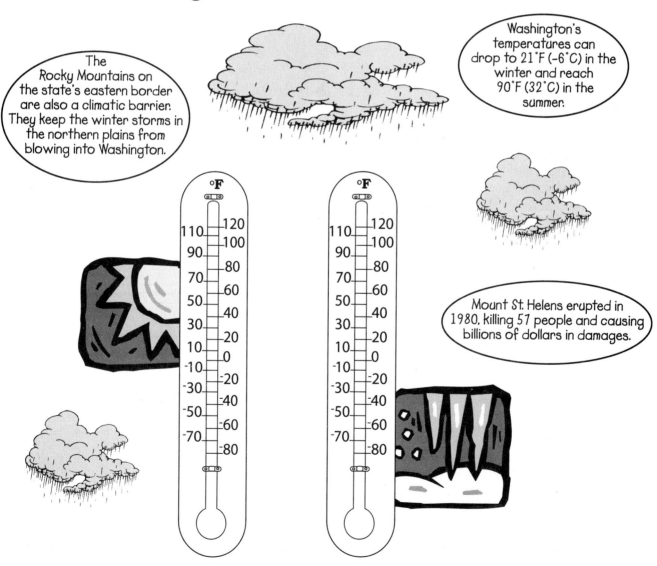

The Rocky Mountains on the state's eastern border are also a climatic barrier. They keep the winter storms in the northern plains from blowing into Washington.

Washington's temperatures can drop to 21°F (-6°C) in the winter and reach 90°F (32°C) in the summer.

Mount St. Helens erupted in 1980, killing 57 people and causing billions of dollars in damages.

The Scenic Route

Imagine that you've planned an exciting exploratory expedition around Washington for your classmates. You've chosen some cities and other places to take your friends.

Circle these sites and cities on the map below, then number them in the order you would visit if you were traveling east to west through the state:

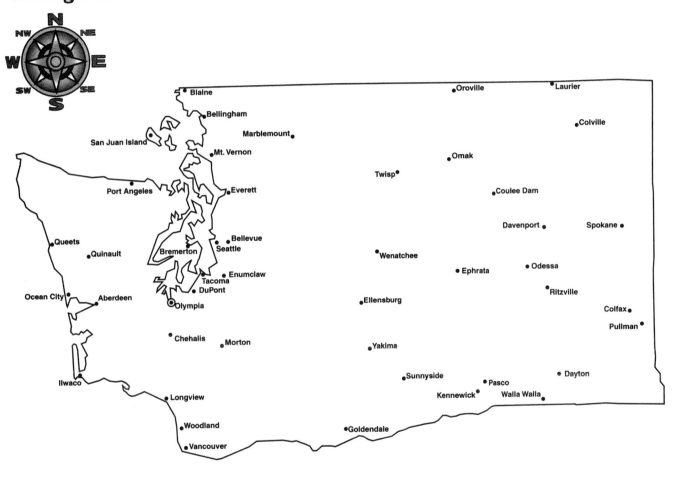

1. _____ Davenport
2. _____ Enumclaw
3. _____ Ephrata
4. _____ Ocean City

5. _____ Odessa
6. _____ Olympia
7. _____ Spokane
8. _____ Wenatchee

Key to a Map!

A map key, also called a map legend, shows symbols which represent different things on a map.

Match each word with a symbol for things found in the state of Washington.

airport
Seattle-Tacoma International Airport

church
Claquato Church

mountains
Mount Rainier

railroad
Burlington Northern Santa Fe

river
Columbia River

road
I-5, 1-82, 1-90

school
University of Washington
Washington State University

state capital
Olympia

Fort
Fort Lewis

bird sanctuary
Skagit River Bald Eagle Natural Area

BROTHER, CAN YOU SPARE A DIME?

After the collapse of the stock market on Wall Street in 1929, the state of Washington, along with the rest of the nation, plunged headfirst into the Great Depression. It was the worst economic crisis America had ever known. Banks closed and businesses crashed...there was financial ruin everywhere.

The lumber industry was the hardest hit in Washington during the Great Depression. Eighty percent of the mills had to close, and loggers' pay dropped to $3 a day.

While the nation was in the midst of the Depression, Franklin Delano Roosevelt became president. With America on the brink of economic devastation, the federal government stepped forward and hired unemployed people to build parks, bridges, and roads. With this help, and other government assistance, the country began to slowly, and painfully, pull out of the Great Depression. Within the first 100 days of his office, Roosevelt enacted a number of policies to help minimize the suffering of the nation's many unemployed workers. These programs were known as the NEW DEAL. The jobs helped families support themselves and improved the country's infrastructure.

The federal government started a dam-building program in the state during the Depression. Work started on Bonneville Dam and the Grand Coulee Dam. The Grand Coulee Dam was considered the "biggest construction job on earth" and provided jobs for 7,000 workers.

Other programs included the Civilian Conservation Corps which provided jobs developing parks, forests, and recreation areas. The Agricultural Adjustment Act helped farmers buy machinery. A program that helped artists and musicians brought folksinger Woody Guthrie to the state to write songs about construction of the Grand Coulee Dam. One of those songs is now the state folk song—"Roll On, Columbia, Roll On."

Put an X next to the jobs that were part of Roosevelt's New Deal.

1. computer programmer _____

2. bridge builder _____

3. fashion model _____

4. park builder _____

5. interior designer _____

6. hospital builder _____

7. school builder _____

8. website designer _____

ANSWERS: 2; 4; 6; 7

Washington Newcomers!

People have come to Washington from other states and many other countries on almost every continent! As time goes by, Washington's population grows more diverse. This means that people of different races and from different cultures and ethnic backgrounds have moved to Washington.

In the past, many immigrants have come to Washington from Europe and Asia. More recently, people have migrated to Washington from Hispanic countries such as Mexico. Only a certain number of immigrants are allowed to move to America each year. Many of these immigrants eventually become U.S. citizens.

Read the statement and decide if it's a fact or an opinion. Write your answer on the line.

1. Many of Washington's early immigrants came from Europe.

   _____

2. Lots of immigrants speak a language other than English.

   _____

3. The clothing immigrants wear is very interesting.

   _____

4. Immigrants from England have a neat accent when they speak.

   _____

5. Many immigrants will become United States citizens.

   _____

6. People have immigrated to Washington from nearly every country in the world.

   _____

An immigrant is a person who migrates to another country in hopes of a better life.

ANSWERS: 1-Fact; 2-Fact; 3-Opinion; 4-Opinion; 5-Fact; 6-Fact

A Day in the Life
of a Pioneer!

Pretend you are a pioneer in the days of early Washington. You keep a diary of what you do each day. **Write in the "diary" what you might have done on a long, hot summer day in July 1855.**

_____

_____

_____

_____

_____

_____

_____

_____

_____

_____

_____

_____

_____

This Old House!

Take yourself back 100 years. Can you imagine what life would be like in the Victorian Era? What did turn-of-the-century Washingtonians own? How did they live?

See if you can pick out which of the following items people at the turn of the century had and which ones they did not.

Circle the things you might find or use around your 1900 home.

H   t Home!

Washin   authors, poets, and other
writers. Here   **their hometowns on the map**
of Washton.

WORD BANK:
Seattle
Tacoma
Wellpinit
Port Angeles
Spokane
Faumont

1. Poet **Audrey Wurdemann** received the Pulitzer Prize for *Bright Ambush*. She was born in the city that is also home to the Space Needle.

2. **Mary McCarthy**, author of *The Group* and *Memoirs of a Catholic Girlhood*, is from a city located across the Puget Sound from Bremerton.

3. **Frederick Faust** wrote under 20 different pen names, including Max Brand and Evan Evans. He is from Washington's largest city.

4. **Frank Herbert**, author of the Dune science fiction series, is from a city between Olympia and Seattle.

5. **Carolyn Kizer**, a poet who won the 1985 Pulitzer Prize for poetry, is from a city in western Washington.

6. **Cartoonist Gary Larson**, creator of The Far Side series, is from a city south of Seattle and north of Olympia.

7. **Sherman Alexie**, award-winning author of *I Would Steal Horses* and *The Lone Ranger and Tonto Fistfight in Heaven*, grew up on the Spokane Indian Reservation in eastern Washington.

8. **David Gutterson**, author of *Snow Falling on Cedars*, is from Washington's largest port city which is located north of Tacoma.

9. Mystery novelist **Raymond Carver** is from a city on northern side of the Olympic Peninsula.

ANSWERS: 1-Seattle; 2-Seattle; 3-Seattle; 4-Tacoma; 5-Faumont; 6-Tacoma; 7-Wellpinit; 8-Seattle; 9-Port Angeles

Washington Spelling Bee!

Good spelling is a good habit. Study the words on the the page. Then fold the page in half and "take a spelling test" on the right side. Have a buddy read the words aloud to you. When finished, unfold the page and check your spelling. Keep your score. GOOD LUCK.

Each word is worth 5 points.

A perfect score is 100! How many did you get right?

Cascades _____

Chinook _____

Columbia _____

evergreen _____

glacier _____

hemlock _____

lumber _____

mountain _____

northwest _____

Olympia _____

Pacific _____

potlatch _____

Rainier _____

rhododendron _____

salmon _____

Sasquatch _____

Spokane _____

volcano _____

Washington _____

Wenatchee _____

Naturally Washington!

Fill in the bubblegram with some Washington crops and natural resources. Use the letter clues to help you.

1. __ ◯ ◯ e __ t __

2. ◯ p __ l __ ◯

3. __ ◯ s __

4. g __ __ ◯ __ l

5. ◯ o __ __

6. __ i __ __ s __ ◯ __ ◯ __

7. p ◯ __ __ t __ ◯ __

8. __ __ ◯ d

WORD BANK
coal
limestone
fish
apples
gravel
potatoes
forests
sand

Important commercial fish in Washington include chinook and coho salmon, halibut, ocean perch, rockfish, and flounder.

Important commercial shellfish in Washington include oysters, Dungeness crab, and shrimp.

Forests make up about 21.4 million acres (8.6 million hectares) in Washington.

The most common species of tree in Washington is the Douglas fir.

Now unscramble the "bubble" letters to find out the mystery word! HINT: What is one way we can help to save our environment?

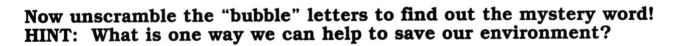

__ __ __ __ __ __ __ __ __ __ __ __

ANSWERS: 1-forests; 2-apples; 3-fish; 4-gravel; 5-coal; 6-limestone; 7-potatoes; 8-sand
MYSTERY WORD: conservation

The Eruption of Mount St. Helens!

The eruption of Mount St. Helens in May 1980 reminded people of the awesome power of nature! A few months before the eruption, the volcano rumbled and blew steam. Huge clouds of ash turned night into day and covered towns with blankets of ash. Places as far away as Montana reported falling ash. Nearly 150 square miles (388 square kilometers) around Mount St. Helens was destroyed and 60 people were killed. Plants and animals have returned to Mount St. Helen today, more than 20 years after the event. It has been designated as a national volcanic monument.

Put these words about Mount St. Helens in alphabetical order by numbering them 1 to 10.

____ eruption

____ awesome

____ nature

____ ash

____ Montana

____ volcano

____ monument

____ national

____ blankets

____ power

ANSWERS: 1-ash; 2-awesome; 3-blankets; 4-eruption; 5-Montana; 6-monument; 7-national; 8-nature; 9-power; 10-volcano

What a Great Idea!

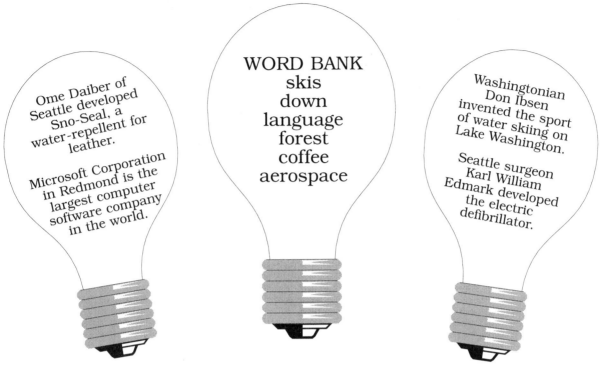

Ome Daiber of Seattle developed Sno-Seal, a water-repellent for leather.

Microsoft Corporation in Redmond is the largest computer software company in the world.

WORD BANK
skis
down
language
forest
coffee
aerospace

Washingtonian Don Ibsen invented the sport of water skiing on Lake Washington.

Seattle surgeon Karl William Edmark developed the electric defibrillator.

There's something missing from the sentences below. Using the word bank, fill in the blanks!

1. Software pioneers Paul Allen and Bill Gates modified the BASIC computer __ __ __ __ __ __ __ __ so it could be used on personal computers.

2. William Edward Boeing was a pioneer in __ __ __ __ __ __ __ __ __ technology.

3. The Kirschner brothers of K2 hold several patents and make __ __ __ __ and snowboards.

4. Howard Schultz is founder of Starbucks, a national chain of specialty __ __ __ __ __ __ shops, based in Seattle.

5. Weyerhaeuser Company is the largest __ __ __ __ __ __ products company in the Pacific Northwest.

6. Eddie Bauer developed the __ __ __ __ jacket after a cold night on the Olympic Peninsula.

ANSWERS: 1-language; 2-aerospace; 3-skis; 4-coffee; 5-forest; 6-down

©2001 Carole Marsh/Gallopade International/800-536-2GET/www.washingtonexperience.com/Page 57

Famous Washingtonian Scavenger Hunt!

Here is a list of some of the famous people associated with our state. **Go on a scavenger hunt to see if you can "capture" a fact about each one. Use an encyclopedia, almanac, or other resource you might need. Happy hunting!**

Bob Barker _____

Bing Crosby _____

Gretchen Claudia Fraser _____

Carl F. Gould _____

Henry Martin Jackson _____

Robert Joffrey _____

Eric A. Johnston _____

Wesley Livsey Jones _____

Steve Largent _____

Phil Mahre _____

Guthrie McClintock _____

Patrice Munsel _____

Craig T. Nelson _____

Vernon Louis Parrington _____

Chief Seattle (Seathl) _____

Tom Sneva _____

Rufus Woods _____

Jonathan Mahew Wainwright _____

James W. Whittaker _____

Adam West _____

Sasquatch (A.K.A. Bigfoot)

Use the words in the circles to fill in the blanks in these Washington legends. Some may be used more than once.

Sasquatch (Bigfoot) are large, hairy, human-like

_ _ _ _ _ _ _ _ _ _ _ _ _ believed to live in Washington's forests and mountains. Sasquatch weigh more than 500 pounds (226.8 kilograms) and are six to eight feet tall (1.8 to 2.4 meters). Descriptions of Sasquatch report the creatures are covered with thick black hair, have a round human-like head, and smell like rotten meat.

_ _ _ _ _ _ _ _ _ _ _ that have been found are shaped like a bear's foot and are more than 18 inches (45.7 centimeters) long. No one has ever found a dead Sasquatch or a

_ _ _ _ _ _ _ _ _.

Native Americans have told stories about the Sasquatch for hundreds of years. According to the stories, Sasquatch look human but don't speak a human

_ _ _ _ _ _ _ _ _ _. They sound more like _ _ _ _ _ _ _ _. Other stories say they sing like an owl and charm people. Sometimes they enter camps or houses and steal food and children.

WORD BANK

skeleton

language

animals

creatures

footprints

ANSWERS: creatures; footprints; skeleton; language; animals

Map of North America

This is a map of North America. Washington is one of the 50 states.

Color the state of Washington red.

Color the rest of the United States yellow. Alaska and Hawaii are part of the United States and should also be colored yellow.

Color Canada green. Color Mexico blue.

Washington has four different mountain regions—the Rockies, the Cascades, the Coast Range, and the Olympic Mountains.

The Channeled Scalabands is a lava plateau that was carved into deep canyons by glacial meltwaters.

The Columbia Plateau is a rolling, prairie-like region in southeastern Washington.

Alaska

Canada

WA

Hawaii

United States

The shoreline of all of Washington's coastline, bays, and islands measures 3,026 miles (4,870 kilometers).

Mexico

N
NW   NE
W   E
SW   SE
S

Officially Olympia!

True or False?!

In 1845, Olympia was settled as the village of Smithfield, which was a shipping port for logging firms. Congress renamed the village Olympia after it was named a port of entry in 1851. When Washington became a territory in 1853, Olympia was named the capital. Olympia is located on the southern end of Puget Sound, on Budd Inlet at the mouth of the Deschutes River.

Read each sentence, and decide if it is TRUE or FALSE. Write your answers on the lines provided.

1   Olympia was settled in 1851.

   _____

2.   Olympia was originally called Smithtown.

   _____

3.   Washington became a territory in 1853.

   _____

4.   Olympia is located on the Olympic Peninsula.

   _____

5.   Olympia was settled as a shipping port.

   _____

ANSWERS: 1-false; 2-false; 3-true; 4-false; 5-true

Washington State Greats!

In the paragraph about important people from Washington below there are eight misspelled words. **Circle the misspelled words, and then spell them correctly on the lines provided.**

Yakima's Phil Mahre was the first American to win a gold medel in men's skiing. He won the slalom at the 1984 Winter Olimpics. Gretchen Claudia Fraser of Tacoma was the first American to win alpine medals. She won the gold and silver medals in the 1948 Olympics. Megan Quann brought home the gold in swiming from the 2000 Olympics. Professinal baseball player Earl Averill of Snohomish was enducted into the Baseball Haul of Fame in 1975. Kirkland's JoAnne Gunderson Carner won more than 40 Ladies Professional Golf Association events and is in the Women's Sprots Foundation Hall of Famme.

_____   _____

_____   _____

_____   _____

_____   _____

ANSWERS: medal; Olympics; swimming; Professional; inducted; Haul; Sports; Fame

Virtual Washington!

It's time to build your own website! We've given you pictures of things that have to do with Washington. Color and cut them out, and arrange them on a blank piece of paper to create a web page that will make people want to visit Washington!

Shorty the Stagehand!

Shorty is a ghost who haunts the Capitol Theater in Yakima. The theater is a live stage and movie theater, like many built across the United States before World War II. Shorty may have been a stagehand. No one is bothered by his presence. He doesn't like rock and roll music. Whenever a loud band is playing, lights go on and off and the sound system goes out. Backstage, there is a door located 12 feet off the floor. No stairs lead to it, and no one knows if there is a room behind the door. It's called Shorty's room, and the door is kept closed. Sometimes, the door is found swinging open!

Read each sentence, and decide if it is FACT or FICTION. Write your answers on the lines provided.

1. The Capitol Theater is a live stage and movie theater.

   _____

2. Shorty doesn't like rock and roll music.

   _____

3. The theater has one backstage door located 12 feet off the floor.

   _____

4. The door to Shorty's room is kept closed.

   _____

5. The Capitol Theater is located in Yakima.

   _____

ANSWERS: 1-fact; 2-fiction; 3-fact; 4-fact; 5-fact

A River Runs Through It!

The state of Washington is blessed with many rivers. See if you can wade right in and figure out these rivers' names!

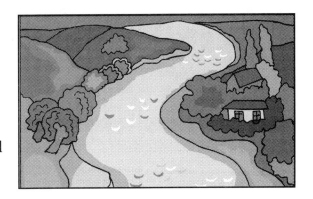

River Bank
Cedar
Columbia
Cowlitz
Grays
Lewis
Snake
Spokane

For each river code, circle every other letter (beginning with the second one) to discover the name!

1. This river is named after an evergreen tree with a fragrant smell.

   B C A E R D Z A Q R

2. River in southern Washington that shares its name with William Clark's partner in exploration

   Z L A E H W B I C S

3. A river that "slithers" through southeastern Washington

   Z S H N C A E K D E

4. River in eastern Washington that shares its name with a city

   A S E P Z O L K B A M N O E

5. River that is the border between Oregon and Washington

   B C A O K L R U B M Z B E I Y A

6. Towns located along this river include Vader, Toledo, Salkum, and Silver Creek

   F C A O X W K L R I S T V Z

7. This rivers name is the plural of the color you get when you mix black and white.

   H G S R X A Q Y J S

Washington Firsts!

Scream for Ice Cream!

The world's first soft-serve ice cream machine was located in a Dairy Queen in Olympia.

#1 Dad

The first Father's Day was held June 19, 1910, in Spokane. It was the idea of Sonora Louise Smart Dodd, whose father raised his six children alone after his wife died.

Fill 'er up!

The world's first gasoline service station was built in Seattle in 1907 by John McLean.

All the Way to the Top!

The first American to reach the summit of Mount Everest, the world's tallest mountain, on May 1, 1963, was Jim Whittaker of Seattle.

Fly Away!

The world's first non-stop flight across the Pacific Ocean ended at East Wenatchee's Fancher Field on October 5, 1931. It started in Toyko, Japan, and took 41 hours, 13 minutes.

Which "first" happened first?

_____ The first American climbed to the top of Mount Everest

_____ The world's first non-stop flight between Japan and the United States

_____ The first Father's Day

Washington Gazetteer!

A gazetteer is a list of places. For each of these famous Washington places, write down the town in which it's located, and one interesting fact about the place. You may have to use an encyclopedia, almanac, or other resource to find the information, so dig deep!

1. Fort Lewis

   _____

   _____

2. Space Needle

   _____

   _____

3. Peace Arch State Park

   _____

   _____

4. Hanford B Reactor

   _____

   _____

5. Mima Mounds

   _____

   _____

6. Albert D. Rosselini Bridge

   _____

   _____

WORD BANK

Lake Washington   Hanford   Seattle
Olympia   Blaine   Tacoma

ANSWERS: 1-Tacoma; 2-Seattle; 3-Blaine; 4-Hanford; 5-Olympia; 6-Lake Washington

Pioneer Corn Husk Doll

You can make a corn husk doll similar to the dolls Washington's settlers' children played with! Here's how:

You will need:
- corn husks (or strips of cloth)
- string
- scissors

1. **Select a long piece of corn husk and fold it in half. Tie a string about one inch (2.54 centimeters) down from the fold to make the doll's head.**

2. **Roll a husk and put it between the layers of the tied husk, next to the string. Tie another string around the longer husk, just below the rolled husk. Now your doll has arms! Tie short pieces of string at the ends of the rolled husk to make the doll's hands.**

3. **Make your doll's waist by tying another string around the longer husk.**

4. **If you want your doll to have legs, cut the longer husk up the middle. Tie the two halves at the bottom to make feet.**

5. **Add eyes and a nose to your doll with a marker. You could use corn silk for the doll's hair.**

Now you can make a whole family of dolls!

Washington Timeline!

A timeline is a list of important events and the year that they happened. You can use a timeline to understand more about history.

Read the timeline about Washington history, then see if you can answer the questions at the bottom.

1792	Robert Gray sails into Grays Harbor and the Columbia River
1792	The coast of Washington and Puget Sound is surveyed by George Vancouver
1805	Meriwether Lewis and William Clark reach Washington and the Pacific Ocean
1810	British-Canadians establish fur trading post near present-day Spokane
1818	United States and Britain agree to joint occupation of Oregon region, including Washington
1846	Washington's boundary set at 49th parallel in a treaty between United States and Britain
1853	Congress creates Washington Territory
1889	Washington becomes 42nd state
1942	Grand Coulee Dam is completed
1980	Mount St. Helens erupts

Now put yourself back in the proper year if you were the following people.

1. If you were happy that Washington became a territory, the year would be _____.

2. If you were worried because Mount St. Helens had erupted, the year would be _____.

3. If you were excited because Washington's border was set at the 49th parallel, the year would be _____.

4. If you were glad because Lewis and Clark had reached the Pacific Ocean, the year would be _____.

5. If you were a ship's captain excited about George Vancouver's survey of the Washington coast, the year would be _____.

6. If you were excited because the electricity generated because of the Grand Coulee Dam brought electricity to your home, the year would be _____.

7. If you were joyous because Washington became a state, the year would be _____.

8. If you were living in Washington when the United States and Great Britain agreed to both occupy the Oregon region, the year would be _____.

ANSWERS: 1-1853; 2-1980; 3-1846; 4-1805; 5-1792; 6-1942; 7-1889; 8-1818

Washington State Economy!

Washington banks provide essential financial services.
Some of the services that banks provide include:
- They lend money to consumers to purchase goods and services such as houses, cars, and education.
- They lend money to producers who start new businesses.
- They issue credit cards.
- They provide savings accounts and pay interest to savers.
- They provide checking accounts.

Circle whether you would have more, less, or the same amount of money after each event.

1. You deposit your paycheck into your checking account. MORE LESS SAME

2. You put $1,000 in your savings account. MORE LESS SAME

3. You use your credit card to buy new school clothes. MORE LESS SAME

4. You borrow money from the bank to open a toy store. MORE LESS SAME

5. You write a check at the grocery store. MORE LESS SAME

6. You transfer money from checking to savings. MORE LESS SAME

The only county in Washington that does not have a technology-based industry is Garfield County.

There are eight national fish hatcheries in Washington, and the state has the world's largest network of hatcheries. I hope I won't be late for lunch!

ANSWERS: 1.more 2.more 3.less 4.more 5.less 6.same

I Am A Famous Person From Washington

WORD BANK

William O. Douglas
Chief Seattle (Seathl)
Henry Martin "Scoop" Jackson
Bob Barker
Arthur Armstrong Denny
John McLoughlin

From the Word Bank, find my name and fill in the blank.

1. I served on the U.S. Supreme Court for 36 years. I worked to protect civil rights and also wrote books on conservation.

    Who am I? _____

2. I was chief of the Native American tribes in the Puget Sound area and befriended the settlers. Washington's biggest city is named for me.

    Who am I? _____

3. I served Washington as a U.S. representative and senator. I was born in Everett, and I ran unsuccessfully for president in 1972 and 1976.

    Who am I? _____

4. I am a television personality and I was born in Darrington. I have hosted game shows such as *The Price is Right,* and I believe in animal rights.

    Who am I? _____ _____

5. I am a pioneer and an author. I founded the settlement that became Seattle and wrote *Pioneer Days on Puget Sound.*

    Who am I? _____

6. I am a Canadian fur trader who founded a trading post at Fort Vancouver. I am a leader of the fur trade in the Pacific Northwest and I helped the American settlers.

    Who am I? _____

ANSWERS: 1–William O. Douglas; 2–Chief Seattle (Seathl); 3–Henry Martin "Scoop" Jackson; 4–Bob Barker; 5–Arthur Armstrong Denny; 6–John McLoughlin

A Plethora (Lots!) of Pictures!

     Washington's Columbia Plateau has many Native American petroglyphs (rock carvings) and pictographs (paintings). There are more than 750 known sites with drawings that date from more than 3,000 years ago to the late 1800s. The images tell the story of the Native Americans' daily life as well as their religious beliefs.

     Ozette Village near Neah Bay on the Olympic Peninsula is Washington's best archaeological site. They used cedar bark to make blankets, hats, and mats. Cedar trees were used to make canoes and paddles. Knives with blades made of slate, shell, and metal have been found.

You are an archaeologist digging at the Ozette Village. Below are pictures of some of the artifacts that you find. **Now, you have to identify these strange objects and their uses. Write down what you think these things are for!**

_____   _____   _____

_____   _____   _____

_____   _____   _____

_____   _____   _____

_____   _____   _____

Washington Native Americans!

When the explorers arrived in Washington, there were several Native American groups already living there. Washington's geography caused two different Indian cultures to develop.

West of the Cascades, the land is rich with natural resources. The rivers are full of fish, and the forests have lots of deer, elk, and other game. The major tribes included the Chinook, Clallam, Clatsop, Makah, Nooksack, and Puyallup. They lived in red cedar longhouses.

East of the Cascades, the Native Americans moved often and lived in dugouts—shelters dug into the sides of hills and covered with grass mats. They fished, hunted wild game, and ate wild berries and roots. The major tribes were the Cayuse, Colville, Nez Perce, Spokane, and Yakima.

Draw a line from the group to its location on the map.

Clatsop   Colville   Makah   Nez Perce

WASHINGTON

Columbia River

Spokane River

Lake Chelan

Spokane ●

OLYMPIC NATIONAL PARK

Seattle

Columbia River

● Tacoma

Olympia ★

MOUNT RAINIER NATIONAL PARK

Yakima River

Snake River

Cayuse

Chinook

Clallam

Columbia River

● Vancouver

Nooksack   Puyallup   Spokane   Yakima

IT'S MONEY IN THE BANK!!

You spent the summer working at Microsoft Corporation in Redmond, and you made a lot of money...$500 to be exact!
Solve the math problems below.

TOTAL EARNED: $500.00

I will pay back my Mom this much
for money I borrowed when I first
started working. Thanks, Mom!   A. $20.00

    subtract A from $500   B.   _____

I will give my little brother this much
money for taking my phone messages
while I was at work: C. $10.00

    subtract C from B   D.   _____

I will spend this much on a special
treat or reward for myself: E. $25.00

    subtract E from D   F.   _____

I will save this much for college: G. $300.00

    subtract G from F   H.   _____

I will put this much in my new
savings account so I can buy school
clothes: I. $100.00

    subtract I from H   J.   _____

TOTAL STILL AVAILABLE
    (use answer J)   _____

TOTAL SPENT   (add A, C, and E)   _____

Wow! Washington Geography Word Search

WORD BANK

Fairfield   Spangle   Monitor
Forks   Starbuck   Mineral
George   Steptoe   Odessa
Greenacres   Yelm   Oysterville
Littlerock   Zillah   Pasco

Find the name of these Washington locations in the Word Search below.

```
O Y S T E R V I L L E M C L M
G S O S Q O A R X I A L F E F
D R C C D D E U O T A E U K D
U C E E S O S T Q T W Y N B Q
G Z S E T A N X F L I Y A K X
I S I P N G P A B E L N E T G
A D E L W A I O O R A H O F E
Q T J X L R C I L O R U M O O
S M B X F A J R D C E V M H R
S L Y I K G H N E K N X D O G
L X E E O G I S W S I Y P S E
N L K C U B R A T S M D S Q G
D S P A N G L E P T J O K D E
P E N H S P K N S K R O F Q E
V B X G I P G G C Y Q I M I E
```

Numbering the Washingtonians!

STATE OF WASHINGTON
CENSUS REPORT

Every ten years, it's time for Washingtonians to stand up and be counted. Since 1790, the United States has conducted a census, or count, of each of its citizens.
Practice filling out a pretend census form.

Name _____ Age [ ]

Place of Birth _____

Current Address _____

Does your family own or rent where you live? _____

How long have you lived in Washington? _____

How many people are in your family? _____

How many females? [ ]   How many males? [ ]

What are their ages? _____

How many rooms are in your house? [ ]

How is your home heated? _____

How many cars does your family own? [ ]

How many telephones are in your home? [ ]

Is your home a farm? _____

Sounds pretty nosy, doesn't it? But a census is very important. The information is used for all kinds of purposes, including setting budgets, zoning land, determining how many schools to build, and much more. The census helps Washington leaders plan for the future needs of its citizens. Hey, that's you!!

Endangered and Threatened Washington

Each state has a list of the endangered species found within its borders. An animal is labeled endangered when it is at risk of becoming extinct, or dying out completely. Land development, changes in climate and weather, and changes in the number of predators are all factors that can cause an animal to become extinct. Today many states are passing laws to help save animals on the endangered species list.

Can you help rescue these endangered and threatened animals by filling in their names below?

1. G __ A __ __ O __ F

2. P __ R __ G __ I __ E __ A __ C __ N

3. B __ __ E W __ A __ E

4. __ O O __ __ A __ D C __ R __ B __ U

5. L __ __ T H __ __ B __ C __ SEA T __ __ T __ E

6. __ R O __ N P __ L I __ __ N

Circle the animal that is extinct (not here anymore).

Washington's State Song

"Washington, My Home" was adopted as the state song in 1959. It was written by Helen Davis and arranged by Stuart Churchill.

"Washington, My Home"

This is my country; God gave it to me; I will protect it.
Ever keep it free.
Small towns and cities rest here in the sun, filled with our laughter,
thy will be done.

(refrain)
Washington is my home; Where ever I may roam:
This is my land, my native land, Washington, my home.

Our verdant forest green, Caressed by silv'ry stream,
From mountain peak to fields of wheat, Washington, my home.
There's peace you feel and understand. In this, our own beloved land.
We greet the day with head held high, And forward ever is our cry.
We'll happy ever be as people always free.

For you and me a destiny; Washington my home.
For you and me a destiny; Washington my home.

Answer the following questions:

1. What rests in the sun? _____

2. What will you do for your country? _____

3. How do we greet the day? _____

4. What is Washington? _____

Getting Ready To Vote in Washington

When you turn 18, you will be eligible to vote. Your vote counts! Many elections have been won by just a few votes. **The following is a form for your personal voting information. You will need to do some research to get all the answers!**

I will be eligible to vote on this date _____

I live in this Congressional District _____

I live in this State Senate District _____

I live in this State Representative District _____

I live in this Voting Precinct _____

The first local election I can vote in will be _____

The first state election I can vote in will be _____

The first national election I can vote in will be _____

The governor of our state is _____

One of my state senators is _____

One of my state representatives is _____

The local public office I would like to run for is _____

The state public office I would like to run for is _____

The federal public office I would like to run for is _____

Did you know that our state government has 49 senators?

No, but I do know we have 98 representatives!

The number of legislators may change after each census.

Washington State Seal

The Talcott brothers designed the state seal. Charles Talcott used an ink bottle, silver dollar, and a postage stamp with George Washington's picture on it. L. Grant Talcott added the words, "The Seal of the State of Washington, 1889." Another brother, G.N. Talcott, cut the printing die.

Color the state seal.

Washington State Symbol Scramble!

Unscramble the names of these symbols for the state of Washington. Write the answers in the word wheel around the picture of each symbol.

1. E W N S T E R   K H E C L M O

    Hint: It grows to more than 200 feet (60.9 meters) tall and its timber is used for construction, boxing, and pulpwood.

2. S T C O A R   D R O N H E N O D O D

    Hint: Its blooms are pink, white, yellow, red, and purple.

3. P E P L A

    Hint: Washington grows more of this fruit than any other state.

4. E A E E L H S T D   T T O R U

    Hint: It is a popular fish for sports fishermen and returns from the saltwater to fresh water to lay eggs.

5. A S R E U Q   C A E N D

    Hint: This dance is known for its figures and footwork.

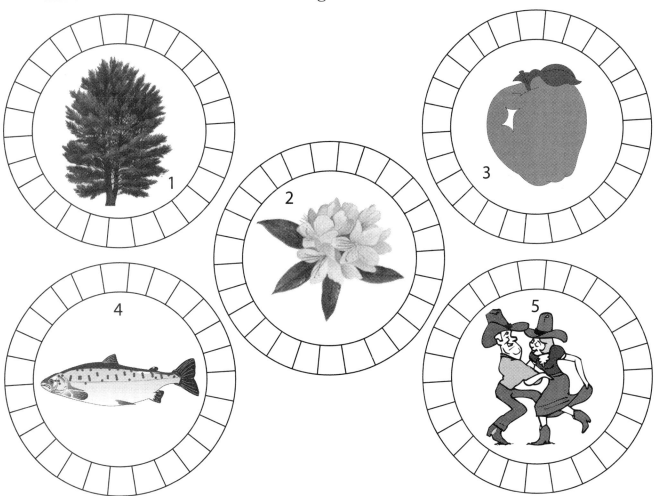

A Quilt Of Many Counties

Washington has 39 counties. Counties are a geographic and governmental subdivision of the state.

– **Label your county. Color it red.**
– **Label the counties that touch your county. Color them blue.**
– **Now color the rest of the counties green.**

Contributions by Washington African-Americans!

They may share their names with U.S. presidents, but George Washington and George Washington Bush made their own important contributions to Washington history.

George Washington was born a slave and was eventually adopted by a white couple, Mr. and Mrs. James Cochrane. The family moved to Washington when George was a young man. On January 8, 1875, George filed his plans for a new town with the territorial auditor. He called the town Centerville. George sold lots to new settlers, and the town began to grow. Later, the townspeople changed Centerville's name to Centralia. George was active in business in Centralia until shortly before his death in 1905.

George Washington Bush was a born a free man in Pennsylvania. He fought in the War of 1812 at the Battle of New Orleans. George Bush and his friend, Michael Simmons, settled north of the Columbia River. They are credited with strengthening the U.S. claim to Washington when the United States and Great Britain were deciding where to put the border between the United States and Canada. His son, William Owen Bush, was elected to Washington's first state legislature and introduced the bill that established Washington State University in 1890.

Read each statement about these important Washington African-Americans and decide whether the statement is a FACT or an OPINION. Write your answer on the line.

1. George Washington Bush and his friend, Michael Simmons, settled the area north of the Columbia River known as Bush Prairie.

   _____

2. George Washington was the greatest man of his time.

   _____

3. George Washington Bush's son served in the first state legislature.

   _____

4. George Washington was the founder of Centralia.

   _____

5. George Washington Bush knew a lot about politics.

   _____

ANSWERS: 1-fact; 2-opinion; 3-fact; 4-fact; 5-opinion

Climbing the Cascades!

Washington's largest mountain range is the Cascades. The range runs north to south through the state and BIFURCATES Washington into two DISTINCT climate regions—the wet and evergreen of the west and the dry, sunny inland empire of the east. The Cascades are also an ECONOMIC and cultural DEMARCATION between east and west called the "Cascade Curtain." The east is mostly rural and agricultural, while the west is URBAN and industrial.

See if you can figure out the meanings of these words from the story above.

1. bifurcates:

   _____

2. distinct:

   _____

3. economic:

   _____

4. demarcation:

   _____

5. urban:

   _____

Now check your answers in a dictionary. How close did you get to the real definitions?

The Inland Empire

When settlers were first coming to Washington, most of them went straight to the Puget Sound area! They believed that eastern Washington, known as the Inland Empire, was too dry for farming. Eventually, the settlers made their way to the Inland Empire and began farming and raising cattle. Cattle ranches are found in eastern Washington, while sheep raising is concentrated in southeastern Washington. Crops grown in the Inland Empire include apples (of course!), potatoes, wheat, alfalfa, barley, hops, spearmint, field peas, hay, corn, asparagus, and onions.

Spokane is eastern Washington's largest city and the state's second-largest. The North West Company opened a trading post in present-day Spokane in 1810, and people have lived in the area ever since. A system of sky bridges, or skywalks, connect the city's downtown buildings and allow for easy walking, even in bad weather.

Walla Walla calls itself the "cradle of Northwest history." Popular attractions include 14 restored, or re-created, pioneer buildings at the Fort Walla Walla Museum Complex. The Whitman Mission National Historic Site, where Marcus and Narcissa Whitman established a mission and were killed by the Cayuse, is located near Walla Walla.

From the Word Bank, find my name and fill in the blank.

WORD BANK

skywalks

Walla Walla

Spokane

Inland Empire

1. I am a city in eastern Washington is known as the "cradle of Northwest history."

   What is my name? _____

2. I am the second-largest city in Washington. People first settled here in 1810.

   What is my name? _____

3. I am eastern Washington. I am home to farms and cattle ranches.

   What is my name? _____

4. You can find me in Spokane. I connect the buildings.

   What am I? _____

ANSWERS: 1-Walla Walla; 2-Spokane; 3-Inland Empire; 4-skywalks or sky bridges

!!! It Could Happen— And It Did! !!!

These historical events from Washington's past are all out of order. Can you put them back together in the correct order? Number these events from 1 to 10, beginning with the earliest. (There's a great big hint at the end of each sentence.)

_____ Gary Locke is the first Asian-American elected governor in the continental U.S. (1996)

_____ Congress approves the Donation Land Law (1850)

_____ The *Columbian*, Washington's first newspaper, begins publication in Olympia (1852)

_____ Permanent capitol building in Olympia is completed (1928)

_____ First library opens in Olympia to serve legislators and territorial officials (1853)

_____ Denny party lands on Alki Point (1851)

_____ University of Washington opens (1861)

_____ American shoots an Englishman's pig on San Juan Island (1859)

_____ Cayuse War begins (1847)

_____ Washington grants women the right to vote (1910)

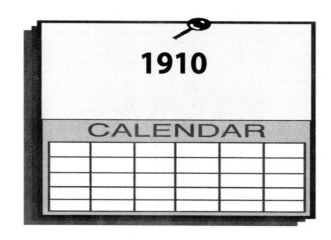

ANSWERS: 10; 2; 4; 9; 5; 3; 7; 6; 1; 8

Riding, Roping, and Rodeos!

Washingtonians love the classic cowboy competition—the rodeo! The best known rodeos in Washington are the Ellensburg Rodeo, held every year on Labor Day weekend, and the Omak Stampede and World Famous Suicide Race held in August. Some people believe the Suicide Race is too dangerous for the horses. During the race, 20 riders ride as fast as they can down a steep embankment, cross a river, climb up the other side of the embankment, then race back to the rodeo grounds!

The rodeos are held throughout the state, but most are held in eastern Washington. Some of the events are sanctioned (approved) by the Professional Rodeo Cowboys Association, which means those competing can receive points for national standing in the event or for the national champion cowboy competition.

Label the rodeo gear.

WORD BANK

chaps
boots
hat
saddle
spurs
vest
lariat
gloves

Washington Word Wheel!

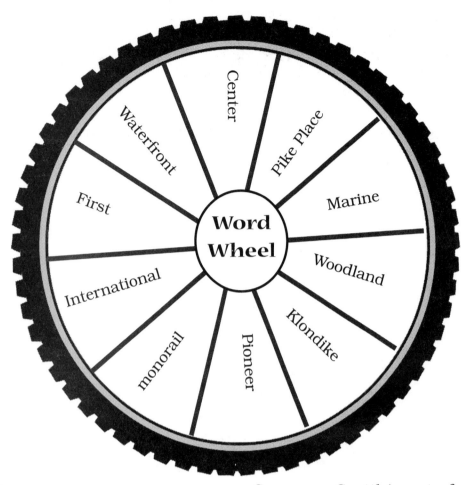

Using the Word Wheel of Washington names, complete the sentences below.

1. __ __ __ __ __ __ __ Square on Seattle's waterfront is the city's oldest neighborhood.
2. Seattle's freshest seafood, fruit, and vegetables can be found at __ __ __ __ __ __ __ __ __ __ Market.
3. Instead of driving your car, take the __ __ __ __ __ __ __ __ from Seattle Center to Westlake Mall.
4. __ __ __ __ __ __ __ __ Park Zoo is home to an African savanna where zebras, lions, and giraffes are found roaming.
5. The __ __ __ __ __ __ __ __ __ __ __ __ __ District is the center of culture and business for Seattle's Asian population.
6. Take a look at Puget Sound's underwater world at the Seattle __ __ __ __ __ __ Aquarium.
7. __ __ __ __ __ __ Hill is also called "Pill Hill" because it's where most of Seattle's hospitals, clinics, and medical offices are located.
8. Seattle __ __ __ __ __ __ is a 74-acre (30-hectare) area built for the 1962 World's Fair.
9. Seattle's role in the Alaska Gold Rush can be explored at the __ __ __ __ __ __ __ __ Gold Rush National Historic Park.
10. __ __ __ __ __ __ __ __ __ __ __ Park goes from Pier 57 to 59.

Washington Pop Quiz!

Pop quiz! It's time to test your knowledge of Washington! Try to answer all of the questions before you look at the answers.

1. Washington's nickname is the
   a. Show-Me State
   b. Gem State
   c. Evergreen State

2. The Lewis and Clark expedition reached the Pacific Ocean in
   a. 1800
   b. 1805
   c. 1776

3. Washington's state bird is
   a. cardinal
   b. spotted owl
   c. willow goldfinch

4. Washington's capital is
   a. Olympia
   b. Chehalis
   c. Walla Walla

5. Which author is NOT from Washington?
   a. Mary McCarthy
   b. Frederick Faust
   c. J.K. Rowling

6. The Columbia River was named by
   a. Charles Barkley
   b. Robert Gray
   c. David Thompson

7. Washington's state tree is the
   a. western hemlock
   b. sugar maple
   c. Douglas fir

8. Washington is the ___ state.
   a. 42nd
   b. 50th
   c. 14th

9. Washington State University is located in
   a. Spokane
   b. Olympia
   c. Pullman

10. Washington's state dance is the
    a. waltz
    b. square dance
    c. swing

Celebrating the Columbia River!

    The Columbia River is Washington's most important river and is the largest river in the western United States. From its headwaters (the small streams that make up the beginning of a river) in British Columbia, Canada, the river flows nearly 1,240 miles (1995.5 kilometers) to the Pacific Ocean. The river enters Washington in the state's northeastern corner and flows more than 700 miles (1,126.5 kilometers) through the state, forming much of the border between Washington and Oregon.

    Dams built on the Columbia River include Bonneville, The Dalles, John Day, McNary, Grand Coulee, Chief Joseph, Priest Rapids, and Rocky Reach.

    The mouth of the river is dangerous for ships and is nicknamed "Graveyard of the Pacific." Shifting sandbars, changing currents, and high winds have caused more than 2,000 shipwrecks and the loss of 1,500 lives.

In each pair of sentences below, one of the statements is false. Read them carefully and choose the sentence that is not true. Cross out the false sentence, and circle the true sentence.

1. Washington's most important river is the Columbia River.
   The most important river in Washington is the Mississippi River.

2. The mouth of the Columbia River is nicknamed "Graveyard of the Atlantic."
   The mouth of the Columbia River is nicknamed "Graveyard of the Pacific."

3. The Columbia River's headwaters are located in Idaho.
   The Columbia River's headwaters are located in British Columbia.

4. The Grand Coulee dam is on the Columbia River.
   The Hoover Dam is on the Columbia River.

5. The Columbia River forms most of the border between Washington and Canada.
   The Columbia River forms most of the border between Washington and Oregon.

ANSWERS: Sentences which should be crossed out—1-second; 2-first; 3-first; 4-second; 5-first

Bridging Washington!

Washington has 78 bridges listed on the National Register of Historic Places, including the Grays River Covered Bridge. The bridge, which spans 158 feet (48 meters), is the only existing covered bridge in Washington and is the oldest in the Pacific Northwest!

The Tacoma Narrows Bridge is one of the largest suspension bridges in the world at 2,800 feet (843 meters) long. The Fred Redmon Memorial Bridge near Yakima is the longest single concrete bridge in North America at 1,366.6 feet (416.5 meters).

The Astoria-Megler Bridge near the mouth of the Columbia River is the longest continuous steel span truss bridge in the world and is 4.1 miles (6.6 kilometers) long! The longest floating span in the world at 7,518 feet (2,291 meters) is the Albert D. Rosellini Bridge over Lake Washington. The second-longest cable-stayed bridge in the world crosses the Columbia River between Pasco and Kennewick—the 2,503-foot (763-meter) Ed Hendler Bridge.

Using the information in the paragraphs above, graph the lengths of the different things listed. The first one has been done for you.

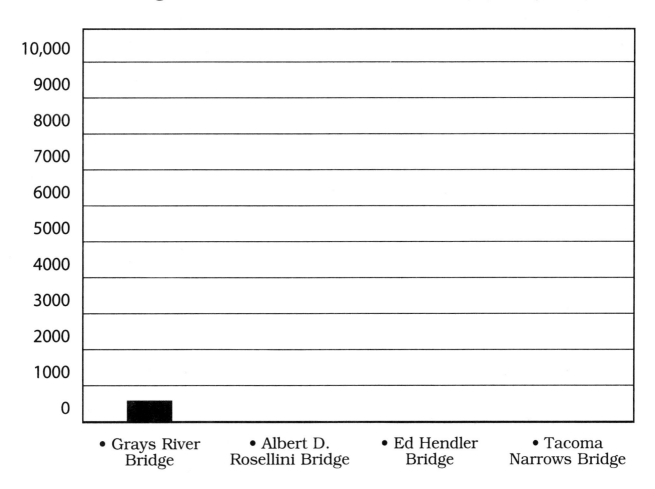

Hoquiam Castle

Hoquiam Castle overlooks the town of Hoquiam on Grays Harbor. Construction of the Victorian-style mansion began in 1897 and was finished in 1900. It was built by lumber baron Robert Lytle and his family, who lived in the mansion until they moved to Portland, Oregon, in 1910. The Lytles gave the castle to their niece, Theadosia Blake, as a wedding gift when they moved. She lived there until she died in the late 1950s.

Now a bed and breakfast, the 20-room mansion has been restored. Visitors can enjoy a great view of the area from the turret, as well as antique furnishings and a 600-piece cut-crystal chandelier.

A *haiku* is a three-line poem with a certain number of syllables in each line. Look at the example below:

The first line has 5 syllables
Beau/ti/ful man/sion

The second line has 7 syllables
Built by a lum/ber bar/on

The third line has 5 syllables
For his fam/i/ly!

Now, write your own *haiku* about the amazing Hoquiam Castle!

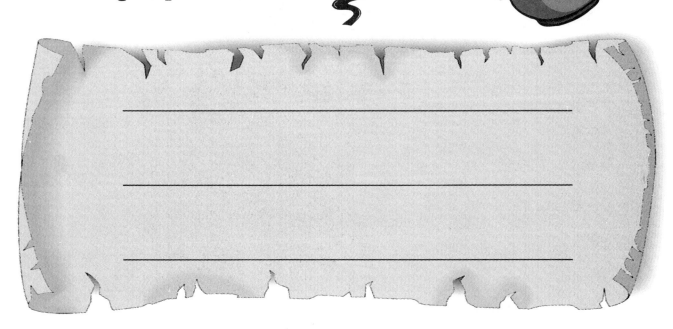

_____

_____

_____

The Marvelous Columbian Mammoth

Did you know school children chose Washington's newest state symbol? The Columbian mammoth was designated as the state fossil in 1998 thanks to a four-year effort by students from Windsor Elementary School near Cheney!

The elephant-like mammoths lived from around 2 million years ago to 9,000 years ago—millions of years after dinosaurs became extinct. Columbian mammoth fossils have been found on the Olympic Peninsula. Studies of the Columbian mammoth fossils have shown that grass was their favorite food. They lived 60–65 years. They were about 11 feet (3.35 meters) long, nine feet (2.7 meters) tall, and weighed about three tons (1.8 metric tons). The longest tusks that have been found were more than 17 feet (5.2 meters) long! The mammoths used their tusks for protection and for digging for food in the snow!

Below is a picture of a Columbian Mammoth. Using the information above, label how long he is, and the length of their tusks, in feet. Then, write how much Columbian mammoths weighed, in tons. Then circle the types of food that Columbian Mammoths ate.

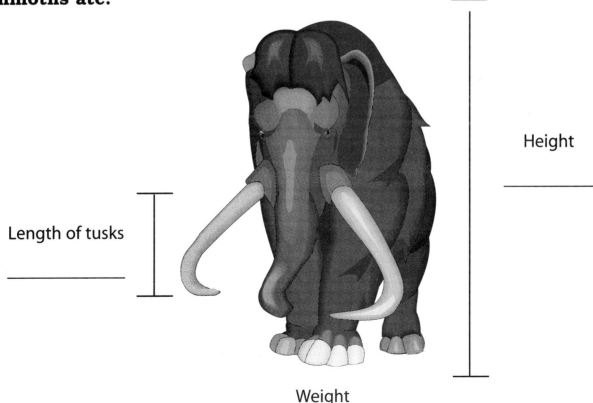

Height

_____

Length of tusks

_____

Weight

_____

How Big is Washington?

Washington is the 19th largest state in the
United States. It has an area of approximately
70,637 square miles (182,936 square kilometers).

Can you answer the following questions?

1. How many states are there in the United States?

    _____

2. This many states are smaller than our state:

    _____

3. This many states are larger than our state:

    _____

4. One mile = 5,280 _____ _____ _____ _____

    HINT:

5. Draw a square foot.

6. Classroom Challenge: After you have drawn a
    square foot, measure the number of square feet in
    your classroom. Most floor tiles are square feet
    (12 inches by 12 inches). How many square feet
    are in your classroom? _____

    Bonus: Try to calculate how many classrooms
    would fit in the total area of your state. _____

    Hint: About 46,464 average classrooms would fit in just one square mile!

ANSWERS: 1-50; 2-31; 3-18; 4-feet; 5-answers will vary; 6-answers will vary.
BONUS: 3,282,077,568 classrooms

Washington Dams

Washington has about 1,000 dams in the state. Dams are built to generate hydropower (electric power generated using water power), irrigate, and to maintain water supplies. Some dams are built for recreation purposes, while others help with flood control.

Most of Washington's dams are considered small (6–14 feet, 1.8–4.3 meters). Intermediate dams are 15–49 feet (4.6–15 meters) and large dams are 50 feet (15.2 meters) or higher. Washington has 91 large dams, all located on the Columbia River. The biggest is the Grand Coulee Dam, which is one of the largest concrete dams in the world at 173 feet (52.7 meters). The Grand Coulee provides irrigation and created the 150-mile (241-kilometer) long Roosevelt Lake!

1. How many large dams are found in Washington?

   _____

2. What dam is the biggest in Washington?

   _____

3. How many dams are located in Washington?

   _____

4. What lake was created by the Grand Coulee Dam?

   _____

5. Name one of the reasons dams are built.

   _____

ANSWERS: 1-91; 2-Grand Coulee; 3-more than 1,000; 4-Lake Washington; 5-(answers can vary) generate hydropower.

Wonderful Washington!

The words below are known as an acrostic. See if you can make up your own acrostic poem describing Washington. For each letter in Washington's name, write down a word or phrase that describes Washington. The first is done for you.

W is for whale of a place!

A is for _____

S is for _____

H is for _____

I is for _____

N is for _____

G is for _____

T is for _____

O is for _____

N is for _____